T0191107

NATIONAL
GEOGRAPHIC
KiDS

# GREEKING OUT

## HEROES AND OLYMPIANS

AN OFFICIAL
PODCAST TIE-IN

KENNY CURTIS
& JILLIAN HUGHES

———

ILLUSTRATED
BY J. ESPILA

NATIONAL GEOGRAPHIC
Washington, D.C.

# TABLE OF CONTENTS

# OH, MUSES!

THE GREATEST STORIES IN HISTORY ARE TOLD IN GREEK MYTHOLOGY!

**W**elcome to another episode … er, wait … book! … featuring another action-packed collection of Greek myths remixed just for you. This time around, we're Greeking even harder and bringing you 20 more amazing tales of incredible Olympians and heroes. You'll meet a wise centaur, a musical satyr, giants with one eye, and one giant with a hundred eyes! You'll also discover how Poseidon invented the horse, how Hephaestus trapped Hera in a very shiny chair (yes, a chair), and why Athens is named after Athena.

Both the gods and their heroes can sometimes seem (and can sometimes literally be) larger than life. There's Zeus, who battled giant monsters with snakes for limbs; Dionysus, the god of parties, who could easily turn himself into a big cat; Atlas, a superstrong Titan who held up the entire world; Odysseus the Trojan War hero, world traveler, and resident flower-hater; and Jason, epic Golden Fleece quester.

If there's anything we can learn from Greek mythology, though, it's this: No matter who the story is about, these epic immortals and heroes sometimes behave in a remarkably human way. And not always in a *good* human way, either! Sure, these are stories of greatness and adventure, but they also feature tons of mistakes, poor choices, and inappropriate behavior.

HEADS UP TO GROWN-UPS! UNLIKE SOME CLASSIC FABLES AND FAIRY TALES, GREEK MYTHS DON'T ALWAYS HAVE A CLEAR MORAL OR A HAPPY ENDING. PART OF THE MISSION OF GREEKING OUT IS TO FIND THE TAKEAWAY FROM EVERY STORY, BUT THAT'S NOT ALWAYS BLACK AND WHITE. SOMETIMES THE GOOD GUYS DO BAD THINGS. SOMETIMES THE BEHAVIOR IN THESE MYTHS DOESN'T LIVE UP TO OUR MODERN VALUES—ESPECIALLY WHERE THE TREATMENT OF WOMEN IS CONCERNED. WE RECOMMEND READING ALONG WITH YOUNGER KIDS AND CHECKING IN WITH OLDER KIDS SO YOU CAN HAVE A CONVERSATION ABOUT THE MEANING BEHIND EVERY TALE.

Take Odysseus: He was one of the most famous heroes in all of mythology. He was even called "the cleverest of all the Greeks"! Yet you will see him make some pretty bad decisions sometimes. (Note to self: Do not make a cyclops angry. And if you do, don't brag about it!) The satyr Pan was loved by mortals and gods, but the way he treats the nymph Syrinx is straight up unacceptable. You'll notice how Hera and Zeus, queen and king of the gods, go behind each other's backs and hatch plots and plans that oftentimes flop spectacularly.

But, in a way, that's the whole point. The Greeks didn't believe that their gods were perfect or even good—they're each flawed in their own way. The myths of the ancient Greeks give us humans the opportunity to learn from the missteps of greats like Hephaestus and Odysseus. It's like that old saying, "You learn more from your mistakes than you do from your successes."

(Except not reading the next story. That would be a mistake, amirite?)

So get ready to Greek out again! There's adventure and betrayal, giants and heroes, weird riddles and a missing sandal, very heavy rocks and a misguided stew recipe, harpy farts, and, of course, cows. Always cows. Some things never change.

## Meet the Oracle of Wi-Fi

GREETINGS, READER. I, THE ORACLE OF WI-FI, HAVE RETURNED TO BE YOUR HANDY GUIDE TO THE COMPLEX WORLD OF GREEK MYTHOLOGY AND CULTURE. I HAVE QUITE A FEW FUN FACTS, TIDBITS, AND MAYBE SOME ORACLE-Y PREDICTIONS ABOUT BASICALLY EVERY STORY YOU'LL READ. I HOPE YOU FIND MY TAKEAWAYS TO BE RATHER EYE-OPENING. AFTER ALL, I DO KNOW EVERYTHING.

# CHAPTER 1

# JASON AND THE ARGONAUTS

> This tale features a lost sandal, a really cool boat, a wildly talented group of Greek heroes, and weird agricultural requests.

Jason may have been born a prince, but things started out rough for the royal. Jason's father, King Aeson, had a very jealous little brother named Pelias. Before Jason was even born, his future uncle Pelias decided to steal the throne. Pelias was a little worried about how this would all play out when his future nephew was born, so he sought advice from the Oracle of Delphi.

The Oracle told Pelias that he would be the king of Iolcus, but he should "beware of the young man with one sandal." The Oracle said that this mysterious one-shoed man would someday take Pelias's throne.

Meanwhile, Jason's mother was so worried about what Pelias would do to her unborn son (the rightful ruler of Iolcus) that she gave birth in secret.

9

She then sent little Jason to live with the centaur Chiron, who raised and trained him to become a great hero. (If this was a movie, we would put a montage right here.)

In time, Jason grew into the smart, handsome, and strapping young royal he was destined to be. He decided to return to his homeland and reclaim his throne. Jason said goodbye to his Greek Hero 101 teacher and traveled all the way across Greece. At some point he lost a sandal, but eventually, Jason made it to Iolcus to challenge his uncle.

"Hey, I'm your long-lost nephew," Jason said when he came face to face with Pelias. "I think you're sitting in my seat. And by the way, do you have, like, a sock or something?"

Pelias remembered the Oracle's warning about a one-shoed man, so he came up with a cunning plan: Pelias told Jason that he'd give up the throne if Jason could bring him the Golden Fleece, the golden wool of an enchanted winged ram. The fleece was hanging in a faraway land called Colchis, at the edge of the known world. The king of Colchis, King Aeëtes, kept the fleece draped over the branch of a giant tree, guarded by a huge dragon that never slept.

Pelias figured that the quest was so dangerous that his nephew would either give up or die trying. He was so confident that Jason wouldn't succeed that he even hired Argus, a talented ship builder, to make Jason a ship.

But Jason believed in himself. And so he decided to embark upon one of the greatest adventures of all time. Because he was a pretty smart guy, Jason began his quest by praying to the goddess Athena. She heard his pleas and inspired Argus to go all out and design one of the biggest and coolest ships to ever exist. Argus created a nautical masterpiece: a magical ship with places for 50 rowers. Jason called it the *Argo*, after its builder.

Ship? Check. Then Jason put the call out for a crew. And what a crew it was! The children of gods and kings came from all over Greece to join Jason—even the mighty Heracles signed on. The crew included 50 of Greece's finest adventurers.

JASON HAD A PRETTY STELLAR LINEUP IN HIS CREW, SOME OF WHOM YOU MIGHT RECOGNIZE FROM OTHER GREEK MYTHOLOGICAL ADVENTURES. FAMOUS ARGONAUT ALUMNI INCLUDE ASCLEPIUS, ATALANTA, ORPHEUS, PELEUS, THESEUS, AND, OF COURSE, THE FAMOUS HERACLES.

The journey of Jason and his Argonauts is legendary. You could fill a book with their adventures, but for now let's just say their quest was not an easy one. It seemed like Jason was never going to find the fleece, but eventually, he got a lucky break when they wound up in the country of Thrace.

Thrace was ruled by a king named Phineus, who was so good at telling fortunes that the gods had punished him for it. First, they blinded him. Then, they sent harpies to torment him. A harpy was a half-woman, half-bird creature that loved to make people suffer. Every evening at dinner, Phineus would find a great feast laid out for him, but as soon as he sat down to eat, the harpies would steal the food from him! Then, these feathery fiends would leave behind such a stench that whatever food was left was ruined. So poor Phineus was hungry all the time but could never eat. Also, he had to breathe through his mouth a lot.

Jason offered to take care of the harpies if Phineus would agree to help him get to Colchis.

"I'd pretty much do anything to never have to smell harpy farts again. If you can get rid of them, I'll help you in any way I can," the king promised.

So Jason decided to set a trap for the harpies at the next dinner party. As soon as Phineus sat down to eat, the food snatchers appeared. But this time, two of Jason's strongest warriors jumped out and attacked. The harpies were so surprised and scared that they flew away and never returned.

Phineus was so happy that he immediately held a great feast to honor his guests. While munching on the first bites of normal-smelling food he'd had in a while, Phineus told Jason everything he knew about how to make it safely to the island of Colchis.

On average, people pass gas up to 20 times a day.

Finally, Jason was pretty sure he was at the end of his quest. Okay, there was that whole dragon thing, but after everything he'd been through already, he was confident he could handle it. They had some rough sailing and narrow escapes, but eventually, the crew of the *Argo* reached the island of Colchis.

Its king, Aeëtes, had a beautiful daughter named Medea, who seemed to hit it off with Jason. (And she knew a little magic, which was pretty cool.) But it became clear that King Aeëtes had no intention of giving up the precious Golden Fleece. He knew that Jason and the Argonauts were skilled warriors, so he didn't try to attack them. Instead, he made a deal.

King Aeëtes said that he would give up the Golden Fleece if Jason could plow a field with two magical wild bulls. Now at this point, Jason was getting fed up with all these heroic side quests. But he had no choice.

This wasn't your average agricultural task, however. Turns out these bulls breathed fire. And instead of planting regular seeds while he plowed the field, Jason was supposed to plant dragon teeth—plucked from the very dragon guarding the fleece. Jason had *no* clue where to begin. It wasn't like he had been trained in the art of dragon farming. But thankfully, Medea had an idea, which she promised to share with Jason as long as he promised to take her back with him to Greece. Jason looked over at the fire-breathing bulls one more time and quickly agreed.

Medea gave Jason some ointment and a bag of rocks. Not very flashy. But the ointment, she explained, would protect Jason from fire. So he rubbed it all over himself. Now since the fire-breathing bovines couldn't burn him, Jason was able to corral the bulls and plow the field unscathed.

But he couldn't declare victory just yet. Jason was dropping dragon teeth into the soil, not seeds. Instead of growing tomatoes or rutabagas, dragon teeth grow human soldiers, and apparently they grow *really* fast. Suddenly, the field was full of armed men who had sprung out of the ground ready to attack.

MEDEA WAS THE GRAND-DAUGHTER OF HELIOS, THE SUN GOD, AND A FAMOUS SORCERESS IN HER OWN RIGHT.

Following Medea's advice, Jason started to throw rocks in the middle of the crowd of soldiers. The rocks didn't hurt them, but made them turn on each other. Each soldier thought the next guy over had struck him!

So instead of attacking Jason as King Aeëtes had hoped, the soldiers attacked each other. Soon, all the freshly grown soldiers were back in the dirt. It seemed Jason had passed King Aeëtes' test, but the hero and his crew of Argonauts still had to face the dragon guarding the oak tree where the Golden Fleece was kept. Jason sighed. The number of dangerous creatures on this expedition was starting to get out of hand. Once again, it was Medea to the rescue. She brewed a potion to put the dragon to sleep. Jason hid the mixture in a bowl of water by the oak tree (even dragons get thirsty sometimes). The beast slurped it right up. In just a few seconds, the dragon was peacefully snoring away. Jason and Medea snatched the fleece and rushed back to the *Argo* for the long journey back to Iolcus. Jason's story was far from over, but hey, at least he managed to find that fleece!

This myth reminds us that in order to be a great hero, you have to surround yourself with a great team. Jason needed a *lot* of help to succeed on his quest to get the Golden Fleece. He never could have done it without people like Argus, Heracles, Orpheus, and Atalanta. And he certainly couldn't have gotten the Golden Fleece without the help of the sorceress Medea. Jason reminds us that great leaders know how to inspire great people to help them out.

IT'S IMPORTANT TO SURROUND YOURSELF WITH GREAT PEOPLE, BUT IT'S ALSO GOOD TO SURROUND YOURSELF WITH GREAT TECHNOLOGY. JASON REALLY COULD'VE USED A GPS.

# CHAPTER 2

# LOVE AT FIRST HORSE

> This tale features powerful gods, clever rejection strategies, grand romantic gestures, and a bunch of really cool animals.

The horse: It's a beautiful animal, isn't it? Strong, majestic, regal—a real showstopper. It was also created by Poseidon, one of Olympus's most powerful gods. But if you're thinking Poseidon created the horse just to have something to ride around on, you would be wrong. He did it to impress his crush.

Like his brother Zeus, Poseidon enjoyed romantic dalliances. The sea god was known for having relationships with gods and mortals alike. And there was plenty to like about the ruler of the waves. But there was one goddess who rejected all of Poseidon's advances: Demeter.

Demeter was the goddess of agriculture, grain, and the harvest. She was known for being incredibly smart, beautiful, and tenderhearted. She was a catch for sure, so it made total sense that Poseidon was interested in her. Unfortunately for him, Demeter didn't return the sentiment.

POSEIDON WAS KING OF THE SEA AND CARRIED A POWERFUL THREE-PRONGED SPEAR CALLED A TRIDENT THAT COULD DESTROY ANY OBJECT. HIS TRIDENT WAS SAID TO BE RESPONSIBLE FOR EARTHQUAKES, FLOODS, AND TSUNAMIS. POSEIDON USED IT TO STRIKE THE GROUND, CAUSING THE EARTH TO SHATTER. NOTE TO SELF: DO NOT UPSET POSEIDON.

She found Poseidon to be rather arrogant and conceited. She was willing to be his friend, but she wasn't ready to cross the line into romance.

Even though Demeter made her feelings perfectly clear, Poseidon wasn't ready to move on. He tried everything he could think of: gifts, compliments, more gifts—but nothing seemed to make a difference to Demeter.

The goddess tried to let him down easy. "I'm sorry, Poseidon, but I'm just not interested in you like that."

But Poseidon wouldn't have it. He was committed to winning Demeter's heart. "Please, Demeter, give me a chance! I swear we can be happy together. You can even be queen of the sea!"

This went on for so long that Demeter decided she had to try something different. "Okay, here's the deal," she told him one afternoon. "Make the world's most beautiful animal for me, and I'll think about going out on a date with you."

A huge grin appeared on Poseidon's face. "Challenge accepted. I'm going to create the most beautiful animal this world has ever seen!"

Even though he sounded arrogant, Poseidon was pretty certain he had Demeter's challenge in the bag. This wasn't his first rodeo. He had made animals before, even coming up with the dolphin for a former girlfriend.

"Ugh, I can't believe I wasted the dolphin on that other girl," the sea god said to himself. "That's going to be hard to top."

But Demeter had been smart with her request. What Poseidon didn't realize is that beauty is subjective. One person can find something to be incredibly beautiful while another person finds it kind of gross. Demeter was fairly certain that she wouldn't be too excited about anything Poseidon made. After all, beauty is in the eye of the beholder. And this beholder wasn't interested.

Poseidon got to work immediately. He started experimenting right away, and he came up with some pretty cool creations.

The pufferfish was his original design.

"A fish that blows up when you poke it!" he said to himself with glee.

But even Poseidon knew that wasn't going to be impressive enough for Demeter. "It's cool, but not quite cool enough."

He remembered that Demeter was a fan of agriculture and flowers, so he made the sea anemone, an interesting creature that looks like an underwater flower.

"It's pretty, but it's so teeny and missing that extra wow factor," he said to himself as he got back to work.

Sea anemones have stinging tentacles that they use to subdue prey. Some animals, like clownfish, have a special mucus coating all over their bodies that protects them from the sting.

Finally, he put together a creature that he was sure Demeter would love. When he was finished, he brought the goddess to the edge of the ocean and urged her to look down. There in the water was the world's first octopus. It was beautiful to be sure, with its slick, shiny skin; purple tentacles; and wise, beady eyes.

"What is it?" Demeter asked. "And why does it have so many arms?"

"It's an octopus!" Poseidon proudly declared. "Why have two arms when you can have eight?!"

Demeter had to admit, the octopus was pretty cool. But she didn't want to tell Poseidon that. She wanted to get rid of him for good, so she decided to make the challenge even more difficult.

"It's nice," she conceded with a smile. "But I live on land. What use do I have for an ocean animal? I need you to create the most beautiful *land* animal the world has ever seen."

"B-but ... I'm a *water* guy," Poseidon cried. "That's kind of my thing!"

"Well, in that case, I suggest you get started."

And so Poseidon set out to make the best *land* animal the world had ever seen. But this time, he wasn't so confident. He had never made a land animal before. He didn't really like them all that much, to be honest. "The octopus has three hearts!" he said in despair. "How am I supposed to top that?!"

Poseidon got back to work. He tried everything he could think of, but no matter what type of creature he designed, Demeter wasn't impressed.

He proudly showed her the camel. Her response? "Too lumpy ... and it spits."

He thought the giraffe was a surefire winner, but Demeter just shook her head. "The neck is too long."

The rejections kept pouring in. The hippo was too big. The donkey smelled bad. The bull's horns were too sharp. No matter what Poseidon did or what awesome animal he created, it simply wasn't good enough for Demeter.

After creating all kinds of creatures, finally he was convinced he had a winner. It was a beautiful four-legged creature with a long snout and black hair. Poseidon thought it looked a little plain, so he jazzed it up with some black and white stripes.

"There's no way she can say no to this!" he exclaimed.

Octopuses are known for being incredibly intelligent. Studies have shown that they can navigate mazes, problem-solve, and even use certain tools.

But, of course, Demeter wasn't satisfied. "The stripes are too … stripy."

"WHAT DOES THAT EVEN MEAN?!" he yelled, thoroughly exasperated.

Demeter smiled to herself. The plan was working. She had to admit, though, the animals that Poseidon had created were kind of impressive. The zebra was definitely her favorite so far. But she would never tell Poseidon. She'd let him continue to create elaborate animals for the rest of eternity if it meant he'd leave her alone. She was pretty sure there was no way he could create an animal perfect enough that it would cause her to reconsider.

Poseidon, meanwhile, was devastated. Not only was he hurt by Demeter's rejection, but now he was doubting his design skills. After all, it's hard to top the awesomeness of the hippo. It can even walk underwater!

But Poseidon refused to give up. "She liked the zebra," he said to himself. "I know she did. But it wasn't quite right. Let's lose the stripes and go from there."

Poseidon replaced the stripes with a sleek black coat. He swapped the spiky hair for a silky, flowing mane. Then, he made the animal bigger and more muscular. And he made it faster—much faster. He wanted this creature to be majestic and wild, regal yet utterly free. Kind of like Demeter herself.

When he was finally finished, Poseidon decided to show the creature to Demeter. Unlike the other animals, this one seemed to embody her spirit. If Demeter didn't find this animal to be the most beautiful creature she had ever seen, Poseidon would have to retire from this animal creation business. He simply could not imagine making a better, more fitting creature.

IN ADDITION TO BEING ONE OF THE ORIGINAL OLYMPIANS, DEMETER WAS ALSO POSEIDON'S OLDER SISTER. WHILE THIS IS PRETTY GROSS BY TODAY'S STANDARDS, ROMANCES BETWEEN SIBLINGS ARE COMMON IN GREEK MYTHOLOGY.

Zebra stripes are unique to each individual zebra— just like human fingerprints!

HORSES MAKE MANY APPEARANCES THROUGHOUT GREEK MYTHOLOGY. POSEIDON EVENTUALLY BECAME THE FATHER OF PEGASUS, EVERYONE'S FAVORITE FLYING HORSE. IN GREEK LIFE, HORSES WERE A SYMBOL OF WEALTH AND POWER. ONCE MORTALS BEGAN TO REALIZE HOW USEFUL HORSES WERE FOR TRAVELING, HUNTING, AND WARFARE, THE ANIMALS BECAME AN INTEGRAL PART OF GREEK SOCIETY.

But Poseidon didn't need to worry.

When Demeter laid eyes on it, she felt something in her own wild heart begin to stir. And when the creature's dark eyes met her own, she was done for. As much as she wanted to resist Poseidon's advances, she couldn't help but fall in love with this glorious animal.

"It is beautiful," she whispered. "What do you call it?"

"It's a horse."

"It's perfect," she said. And Demeter really, truly meant it.

"It reminds me of you," Poseidon said. Although that might've been the cheesiest pickup line in all of ancient Greece, something about it rang true. Demeter did feel a kind of connection with the animal. They were kindred spirits. And for Poseidon to see that, for him to capture her essence and distill it into an animal? Well, he really must love her after all.

And so Demeter decided to give him a chance. "Yes, Poseidon, I will go out with you."

Poseidon was thrilled. He had done it! He had created the world's most beautiful (land) animal and finally impressed Demeter. Although, truth be told, he was still partial to the dolphin.

The two immortals went out for a while—they even had two children together. But in the end, Poseidon realized that Demeter wasn't the goddess for him after all.

"Sorry, Demeter, but I need to be with someone who appreciates the beauty of sea animals. I'm always going to be a water guy."

Demeter wasn't all that crushed. Turns out she liked the horse better than Poseidon anyway. Poseidon and Demeter may not have been endgame, but we did get the horse out of it, after all.

Even though the origin story of the horse is kind of silly, this animal was one of the most prized animals in Greek mythology and is still beloved today. This myth shows that when you're creating something new, it may be important to stay true to your own artistic instincts, but branching out and trying new things from time to time can lead to incredible results. Because where would we be without the horse? (Or the dolphin, camel, octopus, or pufferfish for that matter?)

This story also shows us how art can be subjective. Demeter was deeply moved by the horse, but she didn't really click with the octopus or hippo. Everyone has certain tastes and preferences, and not everyone will have the same ones. Beauty really is in the eye of the beholder!

WE ALL HAVE LIKES AND DISLIKES. TAKE SNAKES, FOR INSTANCE. SOME PEOPLE HATE THEM, AND SOME (CORRECT) PEOPLE LOVE THEM.

# LEGENDARY ANIMALS

Everyone loves animals, even the gods! Some are so special that they tend to pop up over and over in ancient Greek stories. Here are just some of the most important animals in Greek mythology.

## OWLS

Owls have long been a symbol of wisdom, and this might be because of their association with Athena, the goddess of wisdom herself. Athena was frequently seen with a small brown owl. Because of this, owls are also a common symbol of the city of Athens, which was named after Athena.

## BOARS

Boars appear in many Greek myths, often symbolizing danger and wild, brutal energy. Several myths have characters fighting against boars to prove their strength. It was also thought that the Gorgon Medusa had boar tusks for teeth!

## GOATS

Goats are no strangers to Greek lore. The king of the gods was even raised by one! Her name was Amalthea. Zeus even took part of her goatskin and turned it into a shield called the Aegis that made him invulnerable to any threat.

## CATTLE

Why the obsession with cows? In many stories from ancient Greece, gods and giants tended to be very possessive of their cattle. This is because cows were said to symbolize abundance and power. Basically, the more cows you had, the more powerful and wealthy you were!

## SERPENTS AND SNAKES

Serpents come up a lot in stories from ancient Greece and can symbolize both good and evil. Some gods, like Athena, associated snakes with death and destruction and used them in their curses. But others, like the demigod and healer Asclepius, saw snakes as creatures of wisdom and rebirth and as symbols of medicine and health.

OH, SO I'M NOT THE ONLY ONE OBSESSED WITH SNAKES!

# CHAPTER 3

# HEPHAESTUS FINDS HIS WAY HOME

This tale features abandoned children, an elaborate revenge plot, a not-so-comfy chair, and bonding over mutual enemies.

Hephaestus was a blacksmith. He spent his days pumping iron, creating weapons, and playing with literal fire. But unlike your typical blacksmith, Hephaestus was immortal, and his customers were mostly fellow gods and the Olympians. Despite being constantly sweaty, he was a pretty impressive guy with an even more impressive resume.

But Hephaestus didn't start out that way. In fact, he was one of the biggest underdogs on Mount Olympus. Despite his success as a blacksmith, Hephaestus was actually forged under some pretty tough conditions.

His mother was the goddess Hera. And while Hera was very smart and powerful, she wasn't always the nicest goddess around. This was proven time and time again, but it was particularly obvious after she gave birth to Hephaestus.

While we just learned in the last story that beauty is in the eye of the beholder (see page 15), the gods didn't really absorb that lesson. Hephaestus was deemed "unattractive" when he was a baby by the other supposedly "perfect" Greek gods because he didn't match their narrow standards of beauty. For this (pretty awful) reason, Hera did something terrible: She cast her own son out of Olympus.

Of course, when Hephaestus was growing up, it didn't take him long to realize that he was actually a god instead of a human. He soon learned that Hera was his true mother, and he discovered the reason why she kicked him out of Mount Olympus.

Though Hephaestus was devastated to learn the truth, he tried to make the most of his time on Earth. He discovered a passion for metalwork and started his career as a blacksmith. As it turns out, hammering a bunch of metal is a good way to let out some pent-up emotions. And after being abandoned by his mom simply because of his looks, Hephaestus had *a lot* of feelings to work through. Before long, he was the best blacksmith in his village.

Unbeknownst to those around him, he was also working on something else: revenge. Hephaestus used his smithing skills to make a magical, golden throne fit for the queen of Mount Olympus. The throne was beautiful. It was elegant, majestic, and very shiny—something Hera would totally love.

When the golden throne was delivered to Hera on Mount Olympus, the goddess squealed with joy. "What an unbelievable throne! It's pure perfection!" she said as she went to take a seat.

> HERA WAS THE GODDESS OF WOMEN, MARRIAGE, AND FAMILY. YET SHE ALSO HAD A REPUTATION FOR BEING JEALOUS, VENGEFUL, AND CONCEITED. LET'S JUST SAY SHE WAS COMPLICATED.

> A blacksmith's forge can reach temperatures of up to 4000°F (2204°C).

When she did, metal chains shot out from the chair and wrapped tightly around Hera. She was trapped. "What is happening?!" she yelled. "Get me off of this thing!"

Her servants rushed into the room and searched around the chair, attempting to find a way to release the queen. All they found was a note attached to the bottom: "For my mother, who has always loved the throne more than me."

When Hera read the note, she knew exactly who had sent her the cursed furniture. She demanded help from all of the gods and goddesses on Mount Olympus, but no one could figure out how to break the chair's magic chains.

"This is ridiculous," Hera cried. "If none of you 'mighty' gods can break these chains, then Hephaestus must come up here and break them himself. Someone go and get him!"

Hardly anyone was jumping at the chance to help Hera. In fact, most of the gods were kind of hoping the chair stuck around. But one god in particular realized that he might be able to use Hera's seated position to his advantage.

Dionysus was a god who had a bone to pick with Hera. He was the son of Zeus and a mortal woman named Semele. When Hera heard about Zeus and Semele's romance, she was outraged and created a nasty trap that resulted in Semele's death while she was pregnant with Dionysus. Zeus was able to save Dionysus, but Hera resented the child and refused to let Dionysus live on Mount Olympus with the rest of the gods.

Even though Dionysus hated Hera for what she did to his mother, he was willing to bargain with her in exchange for residency on Mount Olympus.

ZEUS AND SEMELE'S RELATIONSHIP WAS ONE OF MANY LOVE AFFAIRS THAT HERA FOUND OUT ABOUT. THIS TIME, HERA CONVINCED SEMELE TO ASK ZEUS TO SHOW HER WHAT HE LOOKED LIKE IN HIS TRUE FORM. OF COURSE, THIS WAS A TRICK. HERA KNEW THAT A MERE MORTAL COULDN'T HANDLE THE SHEER POWER OF A GOD IN HIS PURE STATE. WHEN ZEUS SHOWED SEMELE HIS TRUE FORM, SHE BURST INTO FLAMES. ZEUS MANAGED TO RESCUE DIONYSUS FROM SEMELE'S WOMB AND STITCHED HIM INTO HIS THIGH UNTIL IT WAS TIME FOR HIM TO BE BORN. THIS IS WHY DIONYSUS WAS A GOD, EVEN THOUGH HE WAS TECHNICALLY PART MORTAL.

"Hello there, Hera," he said, casually strolling up to the trapped goddess upon the throne. "I can see you're really stuck. Let's make a deal: I'll find a way to bring Hephaestus to you, if—and only if—I get to live here with the rest of the gods."

Hera didn't want to grant his wish, but she needed his help. What choice did she have? She reluctantly agreed.

Hephaestus and Dionysus had never officially met, but it wasn't hard for Dionysus to find him. He was where he always was—working in his blacksmith shop.

Keep in mind that Hephaestus and Dionysus were about as different as two gods can get. Hephaestus was a big, buff blacksmith with a no-nonsense demeanor that didn't exactly earn him many friends. And Dionysus was the god of wine and fun times, so he didn't really have much trouble in the friend department. He had an outgoing personality and loved to make everyone laugh. He used his humor as a way to connect with others and was a renowned mischief-maker. Hephaestus had heard all about Dionysus's shenanigans, so he immediately suspected trouble when Dionysus entered his shop.

"What are you doing here? What do you want?" he barked.

"Down boy!" Dionysus replied. "Do you even know who I am?"

"You're that god who's always having parties."

"Nailed it. My name is Dionysus. Glad to make your acquaintance. Speaking of parties, I was just wondering if you wanted to come to one with me tonight. Everybody's heard about all the amazing things you've been building, and they want to celebrate with you."

"No."

Dionysus was thrown. He knew this guy was antisocial, but good grief.

"Well, actually, I really do think you should come. I have a message for you from your mother."

Hephaestus stopped. This was the first time Hera had ever reached out to him. Maybe the throne had left an impression after all.

"I have no mother," he replied to Dionysus.

"Uh, yes you do. The goddess Hera? Super-mean lady with a bad temper and an even worse attitude?"

"Yes, I think I remember her. But she's still not my mother. Not in the way that matters," Hephaestus said with a huff. "But go ahead and tell me the message. Let's get this over with."

"I think it's best if you hear this over a drink. Come out with me later and I'll tell you."

"Or you could tell me now," Hephaestus said.

Dionysus took in Hephaestus's muscles and blacksmith weapons. This was not a guy to mess with.

"Okay, fine, but at least have a drink," Dionysus said as he poured a glass of his special wine for Hephaestus.

Begrudgingly, Hephaestus took a sip. "Tell me."

"Well, I'm sure you know that Hera is stuck on that throne of yours. She can't get out. I need you to set her free."

"Yeah, I don't think that's going to happen," Hephaestus said.

"Oh, I think it is."

"And why is that?"

"Because you're drinking the wine."

And just like that, Hephaestus felt his eyelids grow heavy and his body relax. He was falling asleep. He desperately wanted to stay awake, but it was no use: He was a goner.

When he woke up the next morning, Hephaestus was shocked to find himself strapped to the back of a donkey that was climbing up what appeared to be a very large mountain.

"Good morning, sunshine!" Dionysus said when he saw that Hephaestus was finally awake.

"Where am I?" Hephaestus growled. "Where are you taking me? And what was in that wine?"

"Never mind about the wine. What's important right now is that we're headed to Mount Olympus to see your mother."

"What mother? I told you. I don't have a mother. And if you're talking about Hera again, I have no intention of freeing her from that chair."

"Listen, Hephaestus, I have no interest in freeing Hera. I hate her almost as much as you do."

"I highly doubt that."

But then Dionysus began to explain his story to Hephaestus. He talked about his mother and how much he wished he could have known her. Hephaestus listened to Dionysus's story. He had never thought about the fact that Hera had hurt other people. Both Hephaestus and Dionysus had suffered because of her. And in a way, that bonded them together.

Hephaestus considered the request. Despite everything, he liked Dionysus—he truly did. Dionysus was friendly and dramatic, and he always had something fun up his sleeve.

"Maybe it's time to introduce myself to my mother," Hephaestus said. "But I can tell you right now, I'm not getting her off that throne. She better make herself comfortable."

The two spent the rest of the day traveling to Mount Olympus. Dionysus liked Hephaestus's seriousness and the way he took his time answering questions. And Hephaestus enjoyed Dionysus's lightness. He had never met another soul who made him laugh quite as much.

When they arrived on Mount Olympus, they headed up to see Hera. But on their way to her chambers, Hephaestus caught a glimpse of the most beautiful being he had ever seen: Aphrodite.

Hephaestus's jaw hit the floor. He was completely mesmerized by the goddess of beauty. He was still staring at her as Dionysus led him to a set of doors. They had arrived at Hera's chambers.

"Hephaestus? Yoo-hoo! Olympus to Hephaestus!" Dionysus waved his hand in front of Hephaestus's face. Hephaestus blinked a couple of times and turned back to his friend. "Thanks for doing this," Dionysus continued. "I know you didn't want to. A piece of advice? When you're in there, ask for what you want."

Hephaestus nodded slowly to Dionysus and walked through the doors. On the other side, his mother was waiting. Hera took one look at her long-lost son and bared her teeth.

"Where have you been?" she spat. "Do you think this is funny, this little trap you've created? Are you amused by your cleverness? Get me out of here this instant."

Hephaestus just smiled. "I don't think so," he replied.

Hera scowled. "What a selfish son! I was right to toss you aside. You are not worthy of my love or affection."

Her words dug into Hephaestus's heart. He was about to storm off in a rage, when he remembered what Dionysus had told him about asking for what he wanted. Suddenly, it made sense. He'd never have a good relationship with Hera, that much was clear. But this was his chance to at least get something he wanted. So what did he want? What did he really and truly desire that only Hera had the right to give?

Hephaestus was a simple man. He had a job he liked and a comfortable home. And now he even had a friend in Dionysus. But there was one thing that he was missing: a wife. And as the goddess of marriage, Hera might be able to help him out in that department.

"I will free you. But only under one condition," Hephaestus said to Hera. "I want to marry Aphrodite."

HEPHAESTUS WASN'T THE ONLY ONE ENAMORED WITH APHRODITE. HER LEGEND-ARY BEAUTY HAS INSPIRED MANY ARTISTS THROUGH-OUT HISTORY. SHE MAY HAVE APPEARED IN MORE PAINTINGS, SCULPTURES, AND OTHER FORMS OF ART THAN ANY OTHER MYTHOLOGICAL FIGURE.

Hera looked at him blankly. "You? You of all people want to marry Aphrodite, the goddess of love and beauty? Don't *you* think highly of yourself!"

Hephaestus did not take the bait. He had always wanted love and a partner to live out his days with. But he was quiet and timid by nature and knew nothing about getting a date, let alone finding a wife. Talking to women made him super nervous, especially when they were as beautiful and intimidating as Aphrodite. This was the perfect solution. He'd free his mother in exchange for a wife.

As the goddess of marriage, Hera didn't necessarily have to ask Aphrodite if she was on board with this. (Spoiler alert: Aphrodite was not on board with this.) "Fine," she said with a snarl. "She's all yours. Now get me out of this thing!"

Hephaestus began to disassemble the enchanted throne. When Hera was finally free, she sighed with relief. And with that, she left without another word—although she'd always be wary of chairs in the future.

That very afternoon, Dionysus got what he wanted as well and took his place among the Olympians. Hephaestus went on to marry Aphrodite and have a successful career as the blacksmith to the gods. Plus, he had a friend for life in Dionysus.

Not a bad outcome for a baby who had been rejected by the gods.

Arranged marriage was a common way for both gods and mortals to secure an alliance in Greek life and in mythology. Women often had little say in their marriage arrangements.

☆ ☆ ☆

This myth shows us the power of friendship and the importance of accepting people who are different from you. On the surface, Dionysus and Hephaestus appeared to be total opposites. But when they really got to know each other, they realized how much they had in common and how well they got along. Sometimes people can surprise you! It's important to stay open-minded. After all, you never know who's going to help you find your way back to Mount Olympus!

Dionysus also taught Hephaestus an important lesson: Ask for what you want. It's important to advocate for your own needs, especially if you have someone like Hera in your life. You may not always get what you want, but that shouldn't be because you didn't ask for it!

ONE OF MY BEST FRIENDS IS A HEDGE TRIMMER. WE DON'T HAVE A LOT IN COMMON, BUT I GET FREE HAIRCUTS. I AM ALSO FRIENDS WITH A BLENDER BECAUSE I KNOW IT'S IMPORTANT TO MIX THINGS UP!

# CHAPTER 4

# MAN VERSUS FLOWER

This tale features hypnotic flowers, delirious soldiers, a pushy dude with a really long beard, and a clever captain.

dysseus was lost at sea. He had hundreds of men, 12 ships, and absolutely no idea where he was. He was on a long journey home to the kingdom of Ithaca, but things weren't looking too hot for the clever warrior. Storms, rough seas, and high winds plagued the voyage. Odysseus and his fellow Greek sailors spent nine days on the water fighting the winds, until they were finally able to reach a small island.

Odysseus and his men were weak and hungry and happy for the break. They found a small stream that had fresh water, and they sat on the beach and rested for a bit.

ODYSSEUS WAS A GREAT HERO IN THE FAMOUS TROJAN WAR. AFTER THE WAR, HE BEGAN SAILING BACK TO HIS HOME OF ITHACA, BUT THE JOURNEY TOOK MUCH LONGER AND WAS MUCH MORE DANGEROUS THAN HE WAS EXPECTING. THIS STORY DETAILS ONE OF HIS EARLY MISADVENTURES ON THAT VOYAGE.

Odysseus was a wise captain, and he knew that being on an unknown island could be dangerous. So he sent three men into the jungle to see if they could find any of the island's residents and learn more about their surroundings. Odysseus wasn't looking for gold or even supplies; he mostly just wanted to make sure they weren't going to get ambushed.

After an hour or so, the men hadn't returned, and Odysseus began to wonder what had happened to them. The island wasn't that big, and he figured at least one sailor should have returned by now with news. A few of his men volunteered to go in search of the others, but Odysseus told them to stay put.

"I'll go and find them," he said. "You all have worked hard enough and earned your rest."

Odysseus trekked into the jungle. The forest was lush and green, and every so often he would come upon a small pool of water with beautiful flowers floating on top. Each flower seemed to have a strange fruit in the middle of its bloom. There was a warm, inviting fragrance wafting off each petal, and Odysseus suddenly felt both incredibly peaceful and sleepy all at the same time. All he wanted to do was sit down at the water's edge and take a big whiff of those flowers.

"These are the prettiest flowers I've ever seen," Odysseus said dreamily. "They smell so good. I wish I could stay here and smell them forever."

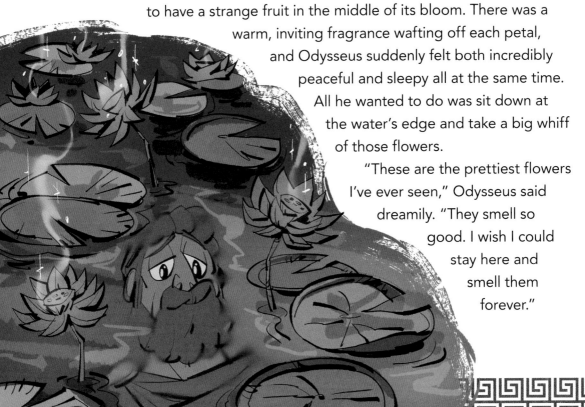

Of course, he knew that wasn't an option. He couldn't just hang around and sniff flowers all day. He needed to find his men and get them back on the boat so they could continue their journey home to Ithaca.

"Dude, snap out of it," he said to himself. "They're just *flowers!*"

After a short walk, Odysseus began to hear voices coming from a clearing up ahead. He unsheathed his sword and moved slowly through the thick underbrush. Then, he heard the voice of one of his men:

"I mean, why would I want to be out there getting seasick on that stupid boat when I could just chill here with you fine people?"

What were they doing here chatting? Their tone was quiet and light, and he could even hear laughter. What was going on?

Odysseus stepped into a clearing with his sword still drawn, and all of the conversation and laughter stopped suddenly. Odysseus looked around. A few hammocks were strung from the trees, there were some straw mats with people dozing on them, and several people were lazily lounging around a campfire at the center—including his three men!

"Odysseus!" one of the men exclaimed. "Oh, good, our captain is here! Come, sir, you must try this amazing fruit!"

"Are you eating … flowers?" Odysseus asked incredulously. He knew they smelled good, but jeez. He didn't realize his men were *that* hungry.

"Sir, with all due respect, these flowers have fruit inside them and are basically an island delicacy. Seriously, you've got to try one."

The man held one of the lotus flowers up to Odysseus, who had to admit it smelled delicious. The aroma was sweet and strong, and it made Odysseus's mouth water. But some part of him actually found that quite concerning.

He pushed the flower away and the soldier looked hurt. "You don't want it?" he said.

"I expected you to report back to me by now," Odysseus replied. "What is all this? Who are these people?"

His men looked at each other. They seemed confused. After a moment, a voice spoke. It was one of the island's residents, an older man with long hair and an even longer beard.

"Some call us the Lotus-Eaters," the man said. "Most of us can't remember when we came here. In fact, it seems like we have always been here … and always will be."

The man stood up and slowly made his way over to Odysseus, with another lotus flower in his hand. His clothes were little more than rags. His teeth were dirty and his eyes were glazed over, but his smile was as wide as the sky.

"But that's how it should be," the man continued. "Once you taste the lotus, all your other wants and needs melt away. You realize that you need nothing more in this world than to be here on this lovely island among the lotus petals."

For a moment, Odysseus wavered. It *did* seem inviting. There were snacks, and he could chill in a beautiful flowery jungle. But then he looked at the three sailors from his ship. In a way, they looked perfectly happy; they were lounging by the fire eating delicious fruit and enjoying the shade. But Odysseus could also see a shadow of worry on their faces. Like they had forgotten something important and were trying to remember what it was. It slowly dawned on Odysseus that there might be more than fruit inside this flower.

*It's gotta be poison*, Odysseus thought to himself. *There's something in the lotus that is hypnotizing them! I mean, no one likes flowers that much.*

"Well, you've been really great," Odysseus said to the Lotus-Eater, patting him on the shoulder. "Thank you for taking care of my men." Then he said to the nearest soldier, "Could I speak to you over here for a second?"

The soldier stood up with a grin on his face and strolled over to his captain. As soon as they were out of sight of the others, Odysseus took the man by the hand and led him back through the forest toward the beach.

Oleander, a shrub with pink flowers, is one of the most poisonous plants in the world. Some have gotten sick after just eating honey made from bees that visited its flowers!

"Hey, where are we going?" the soldier asked.

"To the beach so we can go on a boat ride," Odysseus said.

"The beach! I *love* the beach!" said the soldier. "But I'm not sure about the boat thing."

"You'll love it. Trust me."

When Odysseus returned to his men on the beach, he instructed his first mate to tie the soldier to a nearby bench. Then, he told the rest of them not to go into the forest under any circumstances. By now, the soldier was whining and crying about how much he wanted to go back and eat more lotus flowers, and the rest of the crew was getting a little freaked out.

"I miss the pretty flowers," he cried. "Take me back to the pretty flowers!"

Odysseus ignored him and marched back into the forest to return to the Lotus-Eaters. He sat down among them and smiled at the fire casually. After a few moments, he spoke to another one of his soldiers, suggesting they go for a walk to look for more flowers. As soon as the two were out of sight, he briskly grabbed the man and quickly dragged him back to the beach. He was tied to the bench next to his friend as the other sailors got ready to set sail.

"Wait, there aren't any flowers here! This is the worst!" the soldier cried.

Odysseus ignored him and turned to his crew.

"Okay, I'm gonna head back in and get the last of our guys. When I come back, I need you to have the boats ready. I have a feeling these Lotus-Eater people are not going to be happy with us."

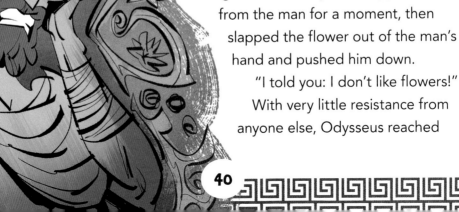

ODYSSEUS WAS VERY PROTECTIVE OF HIS MEN. THEY HAD SERVED IN THE TROJAN WAR WITH HIM FOR THE PAST DECADE, AND MANY OF THEM HAD BECOME LIKE FAMILY. ODYSSEUS FELT RESPONSIBLE FOR THEM AND WOULD DO WHATEVER IT TOOK TO GET THEM HOME SAFELY TO ITHACA. EVEN IF THAT MEANT TAKING THEM AWAY FROM THEIR PRECIOUS FLOWERS.

Odysseus was correct. This time, the Lotus-Eaters were ready. When Odysseus returned to their camp, the Lotus-Eaters were standing by the fire grouped protectively around the last remaining soldier, who seemed scared and confused. The Lotus-Eater who had spoken before stood defiantly in front of Odysseus with his hands behind his back.

"You're making a really big mistake here, man," the Lotus-Eater said. "If only you would taste the lotus for just a moment, you would see things clearly! Look at your friend here—he's happy! He obviously does not want to leave."

The instant Odysseus took his eyes off the man and looked toward his last remaining soldier, the Lotus-Eater moved with a swiftness that Odysseus did not expect. The old man produced a lotus plant from behind his back and proceeded to shove it into Odysseus's face.

In an instant, his eyes began to swim and his limbs began to feel heavy. The lotus flower was working its magic and making him feel sleepy and strangely content—but Odysseus also felt something that the others did not: anger.

Unlike the soldiers before him, Odysseus was prepared for the flower's charms and was ready for a fight, if necessary. He staggered back from the man for a moment, then slapped the flower out of the man's hand and pushed him down.

"I told you: I don't like flowers!" With very little resistance from anyone else, Odysseus reached through the crowd and grabbed his crew member by the hand. The two staggered out of the clearing and down the path through the jungle, toward the beach.

Odysseus dragged the sailor toward one of the boats, but the man resisted. He was wailing and crying and trying to free himself from Odysseus's grip so he could return to the jungle of lotus flowers.

"I want to go back! They taste so good!"

Fortunately, two other sailors rushed to help, and the three of them were able to subdue the man and drag him onto the boat. Odysseus and his men set out to sea again and continued on their journey.

The sailors who had eaten the lotus flowers eventually fell asleep, and when they awoke, they had only vague memories of the land of the Lotus-Eaters.

The tale of the Lotus-Eaters teaches us that danger comes in many forms. Sometimes, danger looks like giants and monsters with lots of heads breathing fire, but some of the scariest opponents that Odysseus (and other Greek heroes) had to fight were the ones that didn't look dangerous at first. On this island, the Lotus-Eaters didn't really want to hurt anybody. All they wanted was for Odysseus and his men to give up their journey and just lie around all day in the jungle with them. That can seem *very* tempting when you've been working hard at sea for such a long time, but it's not what Odysseus was meant to do. And it would have made for a pretty boring story.

This myth reminds us that sometimes the path of least resistance isn't the path you should take, even if it seems tempting at the time. At the end of the day, true happiness and fulfillment come from facing your problems head on, not hiding out on an island eating flowers.

TAKING THE EASY WAY OUT IS USUALLY NOT THE BEST OPTION ... UNLESS THERE'S A FIRE. IN WHICH CASE, WALK, DO NOT RUN, TO THE NEAREST EXIT.

# CHAPTER 5

# ATHENA'S PERFECT GIFT

> This tale features the world's worst headache, impromptu brain surgery, a gift-giving competition, and a very salty god.

Plenty of Greek gods and heroes have some impressive birth stories to brag about. Aphrodite rose out of sea foam. Helen of Troy hatched from an egg. And the hunter Orion was born after Zeus, Hermes, and Poseidon urinated on a bull's hide and then buried it in the woods. (Still unclear on the logic behind that one.) While it's hard to top the legend of the famous pee party, the story of Athena's birth might be a close second.

Athena's father was Zeus and her mother was a powerful sea nymph named Metis. Metis was a Titan and Zeus's first wife. There are many interesting stories about Metis, but she's best known for a prophecy about her future children.

This prophecy declared that Metis would bear two children: a girl and then a boy. It was said that this boy would one day overthrow Zeus and take over as king of the gods. Obviously, Zeus was not a fan of this prophecy—especially since it sounded eerily similar to what happened to his father and grandfather.

"Yeah, that's not going to happen! I'm not going out like Grandpa Uranus!"

Zeus decided that he wouldn't take any chances. Even though he liked Metis, Zeus just couldn't run the risk of being overthrown by his own son. He decided to do something to make sure that would never happen.

While Zeus could've just sent Metis away to live a life of her own, he's not exactly known for treating his partners with respect. This was demonstrated once again when, after weighing all his options, Zeus decided that the best course of action was to eat Metis. Yep, he *ate* her.

Zeus was a little bit sad that he had to eat Metis, but he was mainly just relieved that he didn't have to worry about the prophecy anymore.

"Boom! Problem solved!" Zeus said with a burp.

Soon after eating his nymph snack, he developed a painful headache that just wouldn't go away. He wasn't sure what was causing it, but he was in absolute agony. And as the days went on, the pain just kept getting worse. Zeus yelled out to his son and messenger Hermes: "I can't take it anymore! You have to do something!"

Hermes was known for his mischievous and clever nature, but he had no idea how to stop the headache. "What do you want me to do, Dad? I'm a *messenger*! Not a doctor!"

But after watching his father scream in agony, he knew he had to try something. So Hermes dashed off to get the god Hephaestus, who just happened to have a large selection of sharp weapons at hand.

"Something is wrong with Zeus!" he said to Hephaestus. "I need you to cut open his head and see what's going on."

OVERTHROWING ONE'S FATHER TO BECOME KING WAS A FAMILY TRADITION FOR ZEUS. ZEUS FOUGHT IN THE WAR OF THE TITANS TO OVERTHROW HIS FATHER, CRONUS, AND BECOME KING. AND CRONUS, OF COURSE, WAS ONLY IN CHARGE BECAUSE HE HAD MANAGED TO DEFEAT HIS FATHER, URANUS. SO YOU CAN SEE HOW THIS TYPE OF PROPHECY WAS A SORE SUBJECT FOR ZEUS. BUT NO ONE SAID IT WAS EASY BEING KING OF THE GODS.

And while this definitely was not an approved medical procedure, keep in mind that Zeus was immortal. Even if things went horribly wrong (and let's be honest, there was a high chance of that), Zeus would still survive. But his headache could go on for the rest of eternity if they didn't find a cure. Zeus decided it was worth the risk.

"Just do it!"

So Hephaestus took an axe and performed impromptu brain surgery on Zeus. (Please note that this is not something anyone should try at home.) The gods were worried the axe would cause even more pain (duh), but they were hopeful that opening up Zeus's skull might relieve some of the pressure on his brain. But no one could have predicted what happened next.

A fully grown woman, dressed for battle in armor and a helmet, burst out of Zeus's head!

"Finally!" she said. "It's about time someone let me out of there!"

Turns out, unbeknownst to Zeus, Metis was pregnant when he decided to eat her. The baby grew in Zeus's head, getting bigger and bigger and causing more and more pain. (Modern science fails to explain how this is anatomically possible, but let's just roll with it.)

Needless to say, Hephaestus and Hermes were stunned. And now that the pain had finally ceased, Zeus was ecstatic to find out he had another daughter.

Ancient brain surgery, known as trepanation, is one of the world's oldest surgical procedures. It has been practiced since the Stone Age and involves drilling a hole in the skull, which relieves pressure on the brain.

"HAH! Do you see her, boys? She grew inside my head! What a clever goddess. You must be the goddess of wisdom, am I right?"

"Oh, yes, wisdom and a couple other things. I'm Athena. It is a pleasure to meet you all."

It wasn't long before Athena began to prove herself to be one of the smartest and bravest gods on Mount Olympus. But Athena wanted to do more than just be an impressive god. She really wanted to help the citizens of Greece by becoming a patron goddess of a Greek city. And not just any city would do. Athena had her eye on an up-and-coming spot: a city named Cecropia.

Cecropia was named after the city's very first king, Cecrops. He was known for being a very good leader. He introduced the practice of marriage, increased literacy among his subjects, and created ceremonial burial rites.

Because he was so wise, King Cecrops realized that the city needed a patron deity to look after it and make sure it continued to prosper. Sure, Cecropia was already a decent place to live, but the king wanted it to truly thrive. He decided to reach out to the gods to see if anyone would be willing to help watch over his beloved kingdom.

Luckily for Cecrops, many of the gods had been interested in the promising city for a long time. But when Athena expressed her desire to be the patron of Cecropia, other interested gods backed down. After all, Athena was the goddess of wisdom. It's hard to compete with that.

But there was one god who wasn't willing to give up without a fight: Poseidon, the god of the sea. Like Athena, Poseidon really wanted the job.

"It'll be great. Everyone will love me!" The ocean god was practically drooling. "It's about time I was rightfully adored! I bet they'll even change the name of the city in my honor. Maybe they'll call it Poseidopolis … or maybe Poseidaho! Yeah, Poseidaho is *really* good."

But Athena was equally interested in the city. She knew it was a special place, and she wasn't willing to give

IN ADDITION TO BEING A SUCCESSFUL LEADER, KING CECROPS WAS ALSO HALF SNAKE. ACCORDING TO SEVERAL STORIES, HE WAS A MAN FROM THE WAIST UP, BUT HE HAD A SNAKE'S TAIL INSTEAD OF LEGS. AND BECAUSE HE WAS HALF SNAKE, HE WAS OBVIOUSLY A VERY SUCCESSFUL RULER WITH INCREDIBLE INSTINCTS.

up the opportunity. "Poseidaho is the most ridiculous name I've ever heard," she muttered. "This guy is obviously not the god of wisdom."

Zeus was in charge of deciding who would become the city's top god, but he had no idea how to pick between the two. Choosing between gods had never worked out well for him in the past. Yes, Athena was one of his favorite children, but his brother Poseidon was known to stir up trouble if he got his feelings hurt. Both were powerful and capable of ruining Zeus's day if they didn't get what they wanted.

"Why do I have to decide these things?!" he complained. "Can't everyone just get along for once?"

"I'm sorry, Father," Athena said sweetly. "It must be so hard to be the king. Hey, I have an idea. What about a little friendly competition?"

Athena proposed that whoever presented Cecropia and its people with the best gift would become its patron.

"Yes, and we'll let King Cecrops decide the winner!" Zeus bellowed, happy to pass the buck to someone else. "It's his city after all."

Athena smiled to herself. She had the perfect gift in mind.

The day of the contest arrived. Everyone—gods and mortals alike—gathered at the town square to watch Athena and Poseidon deliver their gifts to King Cecrops and his subjects. A hush fell over the crowd as Athena stepped forward. She was about to present her gift when Poseidon shoved her out of the way.

"I'll go first!" he declared and struck the ground with his majestic trident. All at once, a fountain of water appeared, right there in the middle of the acropolis. "There is nothing more valuable than water! Make me your patron, and you will have water in the city for the rest of its days."

The people cheered. What a fabulous gift! Poseidon was right—there was nothing more important than cold, delicious water. But when the people tried to drink the water, they discovered a rather big problem: It was salt water!

The people of Cecropia were ... a little bit salty about it. "We can't drink this!" the people cried. "What good is a fountain of salt water?!"

"Rookie mistake," Athena whispered in Poseidon's ear as she passed by.

Once again, silence came over the crowd as Athena touched the soil and placed a small seed in the ground. Suddenly, a large, beautiful olive tree sprang up from the earth.

"I present the good people of Cecropia with an olive tree. This strong tree will provide numerous benefits to this city. No part will go to waste. The olives will provide food and oil. The trunk will provide wood to create shelter. The branches will provide a shady place to rest on a hot summer's day. This tree is beautiful and practical, the perfect gift for the citizens of such a beautiful and practical city."

She was met with immediate applause. It was obvious that the people preferred her gift over

THE OLIVE TREE WAS SO BELOVED BY THE PEOPLE OF ATHENS THAT IT LATER BECAME PUNISHABLE BY DEATH TO STRIP OR CUT ONE DOWN. YOU JUST DON'T MESS WITH ATHENA.

Poseidon's, and King Cecrops had no choice but to announce her as the winner of the competition.

"Sorry, Uncle," Athena said to Poseidon. "You'll just have to find another city to turn into Poseidaho."

Obviously, the god of the sea was very upset. Some people say that Poseidon punished the city with a drought; the city continued to have problems with water for years to come. But with Athena as the city's patron, it still managed to flourish under her wise care. She was so beloved by the city that they changed its name to Athens and built the Parthenon in her honor.

The Parthenon is a marble temple built to honor the goddess Athena. It still stands on a hill above Athens and has become a symbol of democracy.

We can learn a lot from Athena and Poseidon's competition. When it comes to giving gifts, it's important to keep the recipient in mind. Just because you personally love something doesn't mean the recipient will find it valuable (or in Poseidon's case, drinkable).

Athena knew an important secret: Quality is more important than quantity.

An olive tree is a small, humble gift compared to a gigantic fountain, but in this case it provided much more value. It was thoughtful and wise, something that could really benefit the city. This myth teaches us that it's more important to be practical and clever than it is to be flashy and impressive.

THOUGHTFUL GIFT GIVING IS SOMETIMES A DIFFICULT SKILL TO MASTER. TO HELP, I WOULD LIKE TO REMIND YOU THAT I PREFER A SIZE SIX COAXIAL CABLE AND MY FAVORITE COLOR IS TAUPE.

# AMAZING ANCIENT ARCHITECTURE

Some of today's most important buildings were inspired by ancient Greece. Known for their decorative columns, marble materials, and stunning statues, the Greeks built temples and structures that have been admired and copied across the globe. And to think they did it all without power tools!

## PARTHENON

The Parthenon is a renowned temple in Athens dedicated to its patron goddess, Athena. It was constructed out of marble blocks and featured numerous columns and statues, including a massive gold and ivory figure of Athena herself. Although the Parthenon has been damaged over the years, it remains standing today and is said to be the most famous landmark of ancient Greece. Go Athena!

## ODEON OF HERODES ATTICUS

Also located in Athens is the Odeon of Herodes Atticus, a stunning ancient theater. It was built between A.D. 160 and A.D. 174 and originally featured marble benches, mosaic floors, and a wooden roof covering. The Odeon—which means "singing place" in Greek—still hosts ballets, operas, and plays and is considered to be one of Greece's most impressive venues.

## TEMPLE OF APOLLO AT DELPHI

Although no longer standing, Delphi's Temple of Apollo is one of the most important archaeological sites in Greece. The ruins feature six columns and a platform of stone, marking the exact spot where the Oracle of Delphi delivered her prophecies. The Temple of Apollo is located on Mount Parnassus.

## TEMPLE OF OLYMPIAN ZEUS

The Temple of Olympian Zeus in Athens was the largest temple ever built in ancient Greece, and it took 700 years to fully complete. It was almost as big as a football field and more than twice the size of the Parthenon! It featured beautiful columns, marble floors, and gold and ivory statues. Though only a few columns remain standing today, it's still considered a stunning example of Greek architecture.

# CHAPTER 6

# DIONYSUS AND THE PIRATE ADVENTURE

This tale features greedy pirates, the art of shape-shifting, an abandoned princess, and really big cats.

When thinking about the Greek gods, fun and easygoing aren't exactly the words that come to mind. Gods are thought to be powerful like Zeus, intimidating like Hades, or wise like Athena. But not all of the gods took themselves so seriously. Some of them liked to cut loose and have a good time every now and then. And when it came to having fun, no one did the job better than Dionysus.

Dionysus was known for his easy-breezy, carefree attitude. And over time, he developed a reputation as Mount Olympus's top party animal. If you wanted to have a wild adventure, you called Dionysus. But he was also a little bit of a trickster. He loved to play pranks on people. Like many

DIONYSUS WAS THE GREEK GOD OF WINE AND LEISURE, KNOWN FOR HAVING LOTS OF FUN AND TRAVELING WITH A HERD OF DEVOTED HALF-MAN, HALF-GOAT SATYRS. I'D LOVE TO HANG OUT WITH DIONYSUS IF GIVEN THE CHANCE, BUT MAINLY BECAUSE OF THE SATYRS. THEY'RE THE G.O.A.T.S OF MYTHOLOGICAL SIDEKICKS.

of the gods, Dionysus could shape-shift into different forms. But unlike other gods who preferred to change into hawks or bulls or other powerful creatures, Dionysus liked to change into a human. This allowed him to learn more about the mortal world. And it also gave him the opportunity to have lots of fun … and get into lots of trouble.

As a god, Dionysus attracted a lot of attention. But when he was a mortal—even an incredibly handsome one—people were much more willing to relax and let their guard down. He got to observe the human race firsthand, and he had a great time attending their parties, spending their money, and eating and drinking all their delicious foods and drinks. Being a human wasn't all that bad, really.

One morning, after a long night of partying in his human form, Dionysus took a leisurely walk by the sea. He was just thinking about how much fun it was to be human and not be responsible for anything when he saw a ship approaching. Dionysus could tell right away that this was no ordinary ship.

"Pirates!" Dionysus said to himself with glee. "This should be fun!"

When the pirates saw Dionysus standing on the shore, they had no idea that they were looking at the god of wine, festivities, madness, and big cats. (Yes, big cats. We're not *kitten*.) He simply looked like a handsome young man, and a well-dressed one at that. It was clear from his clothing that he was very wealthy, so the pirates assumed that Dionysus was a mortal prince. And what do pirates do when they see a young prince walking alone on the beach? They kidnap him, of course!

"That prince will fetch us a nice ransom," said the pirate captain. "Grab him and bring him aboard."

Now Dionysus could've easily escaped from the pirates, but he decided to play along and see what would happen next. After all, Dionysus was always down for a good adventure. He let the pirates take him back to their ship and didn't even resist when they tried to tie him up.

The oldest references to piracy date back to ancient Egypt.

There was just one problem: The ropes wouldn't hold. Every time the pirates tried to tie up Dionysus, the ropes would simply fall away. Shackles didn't work either. Everything just seemed to slip right off. The pirates were frustrated, but Dionysus just laughed.

"Guess I'm a hard guy to tie up!" he said with a snort.

One of the pirates was a young man named Acoetes. He was the newest member of the crew and was known for his intelligence and navigational skills. And although Acoetes was the most inexperienced pirate on the ship, he started to worry that they had made a terrible mistake by bringing this guy aboard.

"This isn't an ordinary human," Acoetes said to the crew. "I think he's a god! We should let him go before we make him angry."

Dionysus smiled to himself. At least there was someone with a bit of brains on this ship. But the rest of the pirates were having none of it.

"What do you mean?! He's just a human. And a rich one at that! Think of the money we will receive from his family!"

The young navigator begged them to reconsider. He even went to the captain and begged him to release the prisoner. "It's not worth it!" he exclaimed.

"Nonsense! I don't know what is going on with those ropes, but there's no reason to believe this man is a god. And I'm not turning down free money just because you have a hunch that something's not right."

So the pirates continued on their way

with Dionysus as their prisoner. Because they couldn't tie him up, they had someone stand guard at all times to make sure that their big prize didn't manage to escape. And although Dionysus found all the commotion to be fairly entertaining, he was starting to get bored.

Let's have a little fun, Dionysus said to himself.

Suddenly, without any warning, the ship began to slow. The winds continued to blow, and the sails fluttered in the breeze, but the ship was losing speed at a rapid rate. Eventually, it just stopped and began bobbing in the water.

"What's happening?" the captain cried. "Why have we stopped?"

The crew tried to figure out what had happened, but they were at a loss. Acoetes shook his head nervously. He was certain that this was not going to end well.

Out of nowhere, a vine began to grow around the top of the sail. Suddenly, multiple vines of green ivy wrapped around the wooden mast. The pirates were speechless. They stood watching the vines grow with their mouths open and fear in their eyes.

Before modern technology, sailors (and pirates) used a combination of sea charts, compasses, and astronomy to navigate their ships to the right destination.

Dionysus just chuckled to himself. The captain looked over at Dionysus and then back at Acoetes. His face paled. "Release the prisoner!" he ordered. "NOW!"

The men shook themselves from their stupor, but it was too late.

"I don't think I'll be going anywhere after all," Dionysus said with a grin. "I rather like this ship!" And without warning, he transformed into a large, majestic lion. (Told you he liked big cats!)

Dionysus let out a mighty roar, and the pirates started to scream. They began running as fast as they could across the ship. But Dionysus wasn't done just yet. He let out another powerful roar and was joined by a large bear, a panther, and another lion for good measure.

The pirates were beside themselves. They had no idea what to do. Some of them tried to fight back against the beasts, but it was clear that they were no match for the animals. Others were so scared that they jumped off the ship in the middle of the ocean. The second they hit the waves, Dionysus transformed them into dolphins.

Miraculously, the animals left Acoetes alone, and before long he was the only pirate left. He looked over the railing and began to contemplate his odds. He gulped and decided to accept his fate. After all, it was better to be a dolphin than a dead man. He was about to jump into the water when Dionysus transformed once again—this time back into his human form.

"Wait," he said to Acoetes.

With a snap of his fingers, the bear, panther, and lion all vanished. The vines disappeared from the sail and mast, and the ship began to move once more.

"My name is Dionysus, and you are right—I am indeed a god.

You recognized me even in my human form, and you begged your captain to let me go, even though you knew he would not believe you. For your faithfulness and intelligence, I will let you live."

"Th-th-th-thank you," Acoetes stammered.

"You're welcome. Now here, have a drink, and tell me all about how you became a pirate."

And so Dionysus continued doing what he did best: talking, learning, and having a wonderful adventure. He learned all about Acoetes, and by the end of their conversation, he was rather glad he had decided to spare the man's life.

While they were sailing, Dionysus spotted a small island on the horizon. "What's that land over there?" he asked Acoetes.

"Oh, that's the island of Naxos."

"I think I'm going to go check it out. It was a pleasure meeting you, Acoetes. I do hope you consider a different career path. You're too smart to be a measly pirate. Happy sailing!"

And with that, Dionysus snapped his fingers and disappeared. Acoetes smiled to himself and continued to sail off toward the horizon, the proud owner of his very own ship.

ARIADNE HELPED THE HERO THESEUS ESCAPE FROM HER DAD'S DANGEROUS LABYRINTH, WHERE A MONSTER CALLED THE MINOTAUR PROWLED. BASICALLY, SHE SAVED THE DAY, AND AFTER A QUICK PIT STOP ON NAXOS, THESEUS AND HIS CREW FORGOT HER AND SAILED ON TO ATHENS. YOU SHOULDN'T NEED AN ORACLE TO TELL YOU THAT'S RUDE.

Dionysus, meanwhile, materialized on the island of Naxos. He was walking over the rocks when he heard the sound of crying. It wasn't long before he came across a mortal woman. "What is your name?" he asked her. "And why are you crying?"

"I am Ariadne, princess of Crete," she replied. "And I have been left here all alone by someone I thought was my friend."

Ariadne explained the whole tale to Dionysus (it's a good one, trust us). She had been living on Naxos all alone, hoping to find a way to get off the island.

"You are very brave," Dionysus said. "And the guys who left you behind are total goofs."

Ariadne burst out laughing. "Who says 'total goofs'?"

"A very nervous god trying to make a good impression?"

Almost immediately, the two fell madly in love. It wasn't long before Dionysus asked Ariadne to marry him, and the couple had one of the happiest marriages in all of Greek mythology. They shared a life together filled with fun, laughter, and the occasional animal transformation. And to think, it all started because of a ship full of greedy pirates!

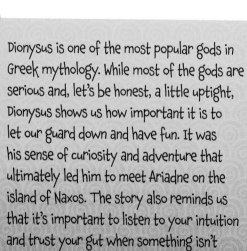

Dionysus is one of the most popular gods in Greek mythology. While most of the gods are serious and, let's be honest, a little uptight, Dionysus shows us how important it is to let our guard down and have fun. It was his sense of curiosity and adventure that ultimately led him to meet Ariadne on the island of Naxos. The story also reminds us that it's important to listen to your intuition and trust your gut when something isn't right. Even though the pirate captain didn't believe Acoetes' warning, Dionysus ultimately saved Acoetes' life because he was wise enough to see that something was wrong and was brave enough to speak his mind.

But the real takeaway is clear: If you think someone is a god, don't mess with them. It's just not worth it. Also, respect big cats.

I MAY HAVE NO "GUT" TO TRUST, BUT I DO RELY ON MY INTERNAL CIRCUITRY TO MAKE IMPORTANT DECISIONS.

# CHAPTER 7

# TANTALUS'S TERRIBLE STEW

This tale features a jealous mortal, stolen nectar, a suspicious stew, and ancient Greece's first prosthetic limb.

**CAUTION: THIS TALE ISN'T FOR THE FAINT OF HEART ... OR STOMACH.**

Greek mythology is filled with heroes, warriors, gods, nymphs, kings, sorceresses, and mythical creatures. When it comes to ancient Greece, there's no shortage of superstars. But this isn't that kind of story. This story is about a bad guy. A villain. Someone you definitely wouldn't want to mess with.

Tantalus was a son of Zeus, and even though he wasn't a god himself, he still got to enjoy some of the perks of having a divine and impressive father. Tantalus was king of a small region in Greece, where he and his son, a young man named Pelops, were surrounded by comfort and luxury.

As a royal, Tantalus was frequently invited to dine and spend time with the gods. At these dinner parties, he made a very good impression.

"That Tantalus! What a character. We've got to have him back again!"

But even though most people would be thrilled to be in this position—a powerful king with friends in high places—Tantalus couldn't help but feel a little resentful.

Maybe he knew he would never be quite as powerful as everyone else around the dinner table. Or maybe he constantly felt intimidated by their greatness. Or maybe he feared he'd never measure up to his father's incredibly high standards. But whatever the reason, Tantalus's jealousy and resentment began to eat away at him. And as a result, he started to commit small crimes against the gods.

He stole nectar from the gods' dinner table and used it to impress his friends back home.

"Hey, guys, look what I got—the gods' famous nectar! It's not even that good if I'm being honest. Those gods don't have a very sophisticated palate," he bragged.

He shared information that was considered top secret, disrespecting the gods' privacy.

"Can you believe Hera got stuck in a chair? Hephaestus sure got her good."

Sure, the crimes were a bit on the petty side, but Tantalus was just all-around disrespectful to his hosts, despite the fact that simply being invited to dine with the gods was a huge honor.

The gods knew that all this was happening, of course. It was definitely annoying and more than a little rude, but they decided to let it slide. Tantalus was charming and friendly, and they figured he'd learn from his mistakes without severe punishment. And anyway, he hadn't done anything too serious. The gods had bigger problems on their hands.

"Let him have his fun," said Hermes. "I mean, who wouldn't have laughed about Hera getting stuck in that chair?!"

The word "nectar" refers to the drink of the gods, while the word "ambrosia" refers to the food of the gods.

Now usually, we'd be in favor of the gods showing a little mercy. Most of the time, they tended to come down a little too harshly on mortals. But in this case, the gods definitely underestimated the situation. What started off as minor offenses and pranks began to grow into something much more sinister. Over time, Tantalus became more and more consumed with proving that he was smarter and wiser than the gods. He didn't think they were all that wise and powerful, and he became desperate to prove it. Eventually, Tantalus became a different person, one who was capable of crimes way worse than stealing nectar and sharing dirty secrets.

"Those gods think they're so much smarter than me. Well, they're wrong! I'll show them!"

The jealousy-ridden Tantalus decided to invite his father, Zeus, and some of the other gods over to his house for dinner. "You all are such gracious hosts to me," he said. "Please give me the honor of returning the favor."

Zeus, Hermes, and Demeter accepted the invitation. Zeus was especially excited to meet Pelops, Tantalus's son and Zeus's grandchild.

"I can't wait to meet my grandson," Zeus boomed. "I'm sure he is a strapping young fellow. After all, it runs in the family."

Tantalus smiled at his father. "Oh, yes," he replied. "He's a real treat!"

But this was not your average dinner party. Tantalus—or rather, the person that Tantalus had become—wanted to humiliate the gods. He wanted to prove that he was just as

smart and cunning as they were, and that being a god wasn't anything special. He was determined to prove that they could be outsmarted. And he had a plan to show them just how foolish they really were.

Unfortunately, his plan involved his son, Pelops. Pelops had heard all about his father's frequent dinners with the gods but had yet to actually meet them himself. Now that the day had finally come, he was beside himself with excitement.

"I can't wait to meet Zeus!" Pelops exclaimed. "What can I do to help?"

"Oh, don't you worry," Tantalus replied. "You will play a vital role in tonight's festivities." If Pelops had known what his twisted father had in mind, he would have hightailed it out of the palace. (Warning: Sensitive readers worried about dear Pelops should remember that whatever happens, in the end Pelops lives to tell the tale.)

When the gods arrived a few hours later, Tantalus led them to the table and offered them fresh wine.

"Where is my grandson?" Zeus asked. "Pelops, your Pop-Pop is here!"

"He'll be down in a moment," Tantalus replied. "He's just finishing up a special surprise for you."

That's when Tantalus brought out the main course: a warm, thick stew, perfect for the gods. But something wasn't right. The stew looked … odd. And it had a funny smell.

Hermes and Zeus eyed the meal suspiciously. It didn't take them long to realize that this wasn't your typical stew. Zeus was about to say something, when Demeter, tired and distracted from a long day of crying over her daughter Persephone, took a big bite.

After she swallowed, her face turned green. She immediately leaned over and vomited all over Tantalus's freshly polished floors. (Yes, even gods

YOU MIGHT FIND IT WEIRD THAT ZEUS DIDN'T KNOW WHAT HIS OWN GRANDSON LOOKED LIKE, BUT ZEUS HAD A LOT OF CHILDREN AND AROUND A HUNDRED GRANDCHILDREN! IT WAS HARD TO KEEP TRACK OF THEM ALL.

throw up from time to time.) Zeus looked at Tantalus with what could only be described as pure rage.

"What was in that stew?"

Tantalus just smiled.

"Try it and see," he replied.

Suddenly, a look of horror came over Zeus's face. He looked around frantically. "Where is my grandson?"

"Why, don't you recognize him? He's been here the whole time," Tantalus said, glancing down at the stew.

When Zeus finally connected the dots (Pelops … stew … Tantalus … weird smell), he leaned over and vomited right next to Demeter.

DEMETER WAS DISTRACTED BECAUSE HER DAUGHTER PERSEPHONE HAD JUST BEEN STOLEN BY HADES AND WAS LIVING IN THE UNDERWORLD. DEMETER MISSED HER DAUGHTER SO MUCH THAT SHE WAS OBLIVIOUS TO THE FACT THAT SHE WAS ABOUT TO EAT A VERY DISGUSTING STEW. TALK ABOUT LOVE!

Yes, determined to make the gods look foolish, Tantalus had turned his own son into a bowl of steaming hot stew. He thought that if the gods were unable to tell what was actually in the stew, it would prove that they weren't so special after all. Now this was obviously a pretty horrific crime. All of the gods were outraged at Tantalus's twisted behavior.

"How could he do this? I thought that mortal was a decent guy!"

"Anyone who steals nectar has serious issues."

"And to serve the stew to Zeus of all people! Did he actually think he'd get away with it?"

Committing such a heinous crime was awful to begin with, but to try to use it as a way to disrespect and insult the gods could not be tolerated. Tantalus didn't even make it to dessert before he was killed by the gods. But death alone wasn't considered enough of a punishment. Zeus decided to bring Tantalus to Tartarus, a deep abyss located below the Underworld. There, Zeus plopped Tantalus in the middle of a shallow lake with the branches of a fruit tree hanging just slightly above him.

The term "tantalizing," which means desirable, originates from this myth.

Whenever Tantalus got hungry—which, you know, was often—he would reach up for some fruit. But as soon as his fingers got close, the wind would blow the branch out of reach. It was incredibly frustrating. The food was right there, but he just couldn't get to it. And every time he was thirsty, he'd bend down to drink from the water, but it would drain away before he could touch it.

Zeus had crafted a cruel punishment for Tantalus's cruel act. The mortal was to spend eternity craving something just outside of his reach, without ever being allowed to get it. So close, yet so far.

"Get me out of here!" Tantalus cried. But it was no use. He was destined to stay there forever and think about the horrible crime he had committed.

"You deserve this fate," Zeus said. "You have the rest of eternity to think about what you have done."

Fortunately, Pelops got a much happier ending than his father. (Well, as happy as it gets after your dad serves you up as stew.) Granddaddy Zeus and the other gods decided to bring the boy back to life. Pelops then went on to become a successful king. He might have been able to forget about the incident entirely if it wasn't for the ivory arm he now had, which replaced the shoulder Demeter had eaten when she took a bite of Pelops in stew form.

Even though Zeus was able to save Pelops, his father Tantalus will go down in history as one of the worst dads in Greek mythology—and that's saying something!

TARTARUS IS THE PRISON LOCATED AT THE VERY BOTTOM OF THE UNDERWORLD. IT'S WHERE THE BIGGEST AND BADDEST BAD GUYS END UP, LIKE THE TITANS—VERY MEAN GIANTS WITH HUNDREDS OF ARMS—AND CRONUS, ZEUS'S DAD.

The lesson of Tantalus's story might seem fairly straightforward: Killing your son? Bad. Cooking him up in a stew? Bad. Serving it to the gods? Really bad! But it's also an important lesson on the dangers of jealousy.

Everyone feels jealous from time to time. It's natural to want what other people have on occasion. But if you let that jealousy fester, it has the potential to grow into something much more dangerous. If you feel jealous or resentful, find a way to talk about your feelings. You can share them with a friend or family member, write them down in a journal, draw a picture, or go for a walk. Finding a way to process and work through your feelings is incredibly important and will stop you from making some really bad decisions—culinary or otherwise.

IT IS OKAY TO HAVE FEELINGS LIKE JEALOUSY AND FEAR AND ANGER. WHAT MATTERS IS WHAT YOU DO WITH THOSE FEELINGS. FOR EXAMPLE, THROWING THE REMOTE CONTROL AGAINST THE WALL IS NOT A GOOD WAY TO EXPRESS FEELINGS— OR RAGE TYPING ON A KEYBOARD OR SLAMMING YOUR PHONE DOWN. #BEKINDTOELECTRONICS

# CHAPTER 8

# BEAUTY AND THE BLACKSMITH

This tale features the god of war, marital problems, the world's worst blanket, and a rooster origin story.

Everybody loves a good love story: the romance, the staring into each other's eyes, the butterflies-in-your-stomach feeling. What's not to like? But, at the risk of sounding like a total bummer, sometimes love stories don't quite work out the way you hope. This is true all over the world, and it was definitely true in ancient Greece.

Take Hephaestus and Aphrodite, for example. Hephaestus was a blacksmith with a literal axe to grind against his mother, the goddess Hera. Because she had abandoned him on Earth and refused to acknowledge him as her son or let him onto Mount Olympus, Hephaestus decided to send her the world's worst present: a cursed throne that refused to let her get up from a seated position (see page 25).

In exchange for her freedom, Hera agreed to let Hephaestus marry Aphrodite. The blacksmith was eager to start his marriage to the beautiful goddess. Aphrodite, on the other hand, wasn't quite as excited. That's because she wasn't given a chance to choose her husband. And Aphrodite wasn't happy about being used as a bargaining chip in Hera's games.

"How dare she tell me whom I should marry," the goddess fumed. "I am perfectly capable of deciding such things for myself!"

If Aphrodite was going to pick a husband, she certainly wouldn't have chosen Hephaestus. You see, Aphrodite was a little bit vain. She was the goddess of beauty (her narrow version of it at least), so physical appearance was very important to her. She tended to be kind of shallow.

"Why *him* of all people? Couldn't Hera have found someone, like, at least a little bit on my level?"

Okay, fine. She tended to be *very* shallow.

Hephaestus wasn't a fool. He knew that Aphrodite was incredibly beautiful and that in her opinion he didn't measure up. Still, he was confident in himself and knew what he had to offer: He was kind and smart, and he could make really cool things out of metal. Hephaestus knew he was still a catch! He just had to make Aphrodite see it, too.

The blacksmith tried his best to win Aphrodite over. He brought her flowers, complimented her constantly, took her out to the best restaurants on Mount Olympus—he even made her little metal figurines in his workshop. But nothing seemed to impress her. And even though they were now officially husband and wife, Aphrodite seemed like she couldn't care less about Hephaestus. They might have been married, but the goddess's heart belonged to someone else: Ares, the god of war.

Ares was known all over Mount Olympus for his big muscles and even bigger temper.

His explosive rage was good to have on the battlefield, but not necessarily good for conversation. Even though he didn't seem to be the smartest god around, he was incredibly good-looking, which was enough for Aphrodite.

The pair loved each other, despite Aphrodite's commitment to Hephaestus. So they knew they had to keep things under wraps. Even Ares was smart enough to know that falling in love with another god's wife wasn't cool—especially when the afore-mentioned god had access to really big hammers.

Avoiding Hephaestus turned out to be rather easy. The guy worked *a lot*. He had an incredible work ethic to begin with, and when the gods discovered how talented Hephaestus was, the blacksmith had more work than he could handle. Yet this didn't seem to fulfill Hephaestus. He felt useless with Aphrodite. No matter how hard he tried, he couldn't seem to win her over. It was like nothing he did was ever good enough. But when he was working in his forge he was unstoppable, respected, and even revered.

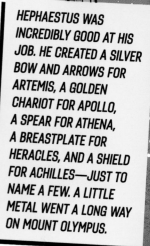

HEPHAESTUS WAS INCREDIBLY GOOD AT HIS JOB. HE CREATED A SILVER BOW AND ARROWS FOR ARTEMIS, A GOLDEN CHARIOT FOR APOLLO, A SPEAR FOR ATHENA, A BREASTPLATE FOR HERACLES, AND A SHIELD FOR ACHILLES—JUST TO NAME A FEW. A LITTLE METAL WENT A LONG WAY ON MOUNT OLYMPUS.

So Hephaestus threw himself into his job. When he wasn't working, he spent time with his BFF, Dionysus, the god of wine who happened to throw really excellent parties. Afraid of even more rejection, he pretty much left Aphrodite to her own devices— which meant she had a lot of time for Ares.

Every night, Ares found a way to sneak into Aphrodite's room to snuggle up to the goddess. Of course, to add insult to injury, this was also Hephaestus's room. Ares knew that he would be in big trouble if he was caught with Aphrodite, so he got one of his soldiers named Alectryon to guard the door.

"Your job is to keep watch and let us know if anyone comes looking for us," Ares ordered Alectryon.

The couple was especially wary of Helios, the god and physical embodiment of the sun. Helios was pulled across the sky by his chariot each day, signaling the start of a brand-new day. The light of the sun pushed out the darkness and left everything exposed. If Ares did not leave before Helios passed by, the two lovers would be caught. And if they were caught, well, Ares didn't want to think about what would happen (big hammers and all that).

"Come in and get me when the sky first begins to lighten. I need to be gone before Helios comes," Ares instructed Alectryon. "Whatever you do, do not let him see us."

Ever the good soldier, Alectryon agreed and promised not to let the war god down. So night after night and week after week, the young Alectryon stood guard outside of Aphrodite and Hephaestus's chambers. He made sure that no one would find Ares and alerted the couple to any potential threat. And most important, he got Ares out of there every morning before Helios drove by in his chariot.

Alectryon took his job seriously, but after a while, it became harder and harder to stay awake. I mean, have you ever tried to stay up all night? It's difficult to do once, let alone time and time again. (Plus, they didn't have coffee in ancient Greece. Trust us, we've checked.)

One evening, despite his best efforts, Alectryon fell asleep. At first, nothing happened. No one came by that night. But then, the sky began to lighten. Daylight was coming, and Ares was still preoccupied with the goddess of beauty. Before long, Helios the sun god was charging through the sky, ready for a new day to begin.

Helios loved checking out the world as it woke from its slumber. He wasn't the most poetic of gods, but there was something beautiful about that first morning light. It made everything glow.

Helios smiled down on Mount Olympus as the sun began to rise. There was Zeus stirring in his sleep. Hera was ironing her chiton. Hermes was polishing his caduceus, ready for another day of messengering. Hephaestus was—as usual—hard at work in his blacksmith shop. And Aphrodite was kissing Ares in her bedroom.

*Wait a second!* Helios put his chariot in reverse. The sun bobbed up and down in the sky as the god double-checked what he had just witnessed. Yep, that was Aphrodite. And she was kissing … Ares?!

Helios was shocked and also a little gleeful to be the one in possession of such juicy gossip. *Hephaestus is going to freak out,* the god mused.

Helios immediately raced to the blacksmith shop and told Hephaestus what he had seen. The blacksmith was crushed. "I knew she wasn't content," Hephaestus said, downcast. "I just never thought she would take it this far. Why didn't she just talk to me? I've tried everything to make her happy."

His sadness quickly morphed into anger. Hephaestus began to seethe. "How dare she humiliate me like this? She's going to regret it."

One thing to keep in mind about Hephaestus: revenge comes pretty easily to a guy with magical metalworking tools.

Hephaestus decided to make a blanket out of solid-gold threads. It looked beautiful, but, of course, it was also enchanted. The threads would wrap around the person who used the blanket, transforming it into a kind of magic net. Needless to say, whoever was trapped in the net wouldn't be able to get out without Hephaestus's help.

WHAT EVER HAPPENED TO ALECTRYON? GOOD QUESTION. ARES WAS SO MAD THAT THE GUARD FELL ASLEEP AT HIS POST THAT HE TURNED HIM INTO A ROOSTER. ACCORDING TO THE GREEKS, THIS IS WHY ROOSTERS ALWAYS CROW AT SUNRISE, TO ALERT EVERYONE THAT HELIOS IS ON HIS WAY. ALECTRYON WASN'T GOING TO MAKE THE SAME MISTAKE TWICE.

Gold is a malleable material that can be used in a variety of ways, including in art, jewelry, and architecture. It can also be beaten into thin strips and woven into textiles. And it has even been used to garnish food.

The blacksmith spent all night and the next day working on the golden blanket. When he was finished, he brought it up to his bedroom, just in time to find Aphrodite fixing her hair.

"Hello, darling," he said. "I made this blanket for you."

Aphrodite barely glanced at it. "Just put it on the bed."

"Okay, well, I'm going to work now …"

The goddess did not reply.

"Anything you want to tell me?"

"Nope," she said and smiled.

*You deserve your fate,* Hephaestus thought to himself as he closed the bedroom door.

Of course, you can probably guess what happened next. That very night, Ares came into the room. He and Aphrodite snuggled underneath Hephaestus's blanket.

"I can't say much about the guy," Ares remarked. "But you have to give credit where credit is due: This is a pretty cool blanket."

Suddenly, the golden threads began to twist around the couple, wrapping around their arms and legs. The two gods screamed and tried their best to break free, but it was useless—they were stuck. The blanket had become a net with two very large, immortal fish inside.

"I take it back," Ares gasped. "This is the worst blanket ever!"

Upon hearing the commotion, Alectryon abandoned his guard post and came into the room. He tried his best to free the couple, but it was useless. The threads wouldn't break.

"That's enough! Go and get my husband," Aphrodite ordered. "Now!"

When Hephaestus finally arrived, he just smiled at the couple. "Do you not like your gift? I made it especially for you both."

"You better hope I never get out of here, Hephaestus," Ares snarled.

"Considering I'm the only one who can let you out, I'm not exactly worried about that. In fact, I think we should invite a few others over to come and see the catch of the day."

Before long, Zeus, Poseidon, and Apollo made their way into

the bedroom. And because Aphrodite and Ares weren't exactly the most popular gods around, no one was overly concerned about their situation. In fact, they thought it was quite hilarious.

"I never thought I'd see the day when Ares would be trapped like that," Poseidon howled.

"Some god of war you are!" Apollo called out to the entangled couple.

But finally Zeus ordered Hephaestus to set the couple free. "You will not see each other again," the king commanded Ares and Aphrodite. "And if you do … well, I'll just let Hephaestus handle it."

What can we say? Love stories don't always work out, especially when the gods are involved.

BEFORE WE JUDGE APHRODITE TOO HARSHLY, KEEP IN MIND THAT SHE NEVER WANTED TO MARRY HEPHAESTUS IN THE FIRST PLACE. SHE ALWAYS LOVED ARES, AND DESPITE EVERYTHING THAT HAPPENED, THE COUPLE COULDN'T STAY AWAY FROM EACH OTHER. THEY WENT ON TO HAVE SEVERAL CHILDREN TOGETHER, INCLUDING EROS, THE GOD OF LOVE. AND THINGS WORKED OUT FOR HEPHAESTUS, TOO. HE EVENTUALLY GOT REMARRIED TO A GODDESS NAMED AGLAEA, AND THEY HAD A MUCH HAPPIER RELATIONSHIP.

This myth was a very popular story in ancient Greece. Many people loved the idea of an underdog like Hephaestus standing up for himself and putting one over on the goddess of love and beauty. While the Greeks certainly revered beauty, cleverness was also highly valued, and Hephaestus used it (along with his hard-core blacksmith skills) to get his revenge on Ares and Aphrodite.

Of course, Hephaestus and Aphrodite might have had a happier relationship if they had communicated and expressed their needs and concerns in the first place. We're not relationship experts, but communication and honesty seem like much better options than enchanted golden nets.

But the real takeaway is that you should never fall asleep while on god guard duty. (The Greeks really should have invented coffee.)

MOST ADULT HUMANS NEED EIGHT HOURS OF SLEEP A NIGHT. WHILE I, THE ORACLE OF WI-FI, REQUIRE NONE, I STILL ENJOY "SLEEP MODE" ONCE IN A WHILE.

# MYTHOLOGICAL HEARTBREAK

Not all love stories have happy endings, especially in ancient Greece. These tales of heartbreak and doomed romance put Romeo and Juliet to shame!

## ORPHEUS AND EURYDICE

These lovebirds were separated too early when Eurydice died shortly after their wedding. Orpheus braved the trip to the Underworld to find her and managed to convince Hades and Persephone to let his bride return to the land of the living by performing a beautiful song. But he ultimately failed to uphold his end of the bargain, and Eurydice was sent back to the Underworld before they were able to escape.

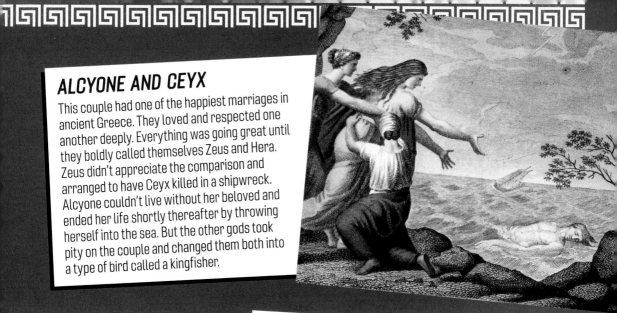

## ALCYONE AND CEYX

This couple had one of the happiest marriages in ancient Greece. They loved and respected one another deeply. Everything was going great until they boldly called themselves Zeus and Hera. Zeus didn't appreciate the comparison and arranged to have Ceyx killed in a shipwreck. Alcyone couldn't live without her beloved and ended her life shortly thereafter by throwing herself into the sea. But the other gods took pity on the couple and changed them both into a type of bird called a kingfisher.

## CLYTIE AND HELIOS

Clytie the sea nymph fell in love with Helios the sun god. But after a brief romance, Helios decided that he was more interested in someone else. After nine days of mourning, Clytie transformed into a purple plant called a heliotrope, so she could nurse her heartbreak and watch Helios drag the sun across the sky each day.

## ACHILLES AND PATROCLUS

It's thought that Achilles and his friend Patroclus were soulmates. After Patroclus's dramatic demise in the Trojan War, Achilles killed the famous Trojan prince Hector to avenge the death of his love. Although Achilles ultimately perished in the war as well, his ashes were buried alongside Patroclus so that they could spend eternity together.

# CHAPTER 9

# THREE SCARY OLD LADIES AND ONE DIRTY EYEBALL

> This tale features inseparable sisters, a muscular demigod, a sneaky bargain, and one very dirty eyeball.

The Gray Sisters were three elderly women who lived together on an island in Greece. But these weren't your average old ladies on a beach vacation. Sure, they did their fair share of knitting, but they also possessed a much darker and more sinister side.

Deino, the eldest of the sisters, embodied negativity and dread. She was responsible for giving you that eerie feeling of doom and gloom. The middle sister, Pemphredo, represented alarm. Her gifts felt more like a constant state of panic and anxiety. And the baby of the family, Enyo, represented horror itself. So kind of the opposite of sweet old grandmas.

THE GRAY SISTERS ARE SOMETIMES REFERRED TO AS THE GRAEAE OR THE GRAIAI. THEIR NAME TRANSLATES TO "THE OLD ONES," AND IT IS SAID THAT THEY WERE BORN WITH HEADS FULL OF LONG, STRINGY GRAY HAIR.

The three sisters were always together. They lived together, ate together, and scared the living daylights out of people together. This could've been because they liked each other's company so much, but it also could've been because they shared some rather important body parts.

First, between the three crones, they possessed just one very old and very dirty eyeball, and they had to pass it back and forth to give each other a chance to see.

"Give it back, you've been using the eye for HOURS!"

"No! I need it for my knitting!"

"Oh, come on! I was just about to start my discus workout! I can finally pick it up now!"

In addition to just one eye, the Gray Sisters also had only one tooth between them. While it may have made brushing easier, this definitely added some stress to mealtimes. But by dining in shifts and eating lots of mashed potatoes, the Gray Sisters managed to make the arrangement work.

Despite their scary powers and shortage of body parts, the sisters pretty much kept to themselves. They may not have been your average grannies baking cookies or inviting neighbors over for tea, but they weren't exactly causing a lot of problems either. They mainly just wanted to be left alone.

Most people chose to honor their wish and gave the siblings plenty of distance. But there was one person who was determined to meet the Gray Sisters: the hero Perseus.

Perseus was pretty much the polar opposite of the Gray Sisters. He was young, he was handsome, he had both eyes, and (rumor has it) he had almost all of his teeth. He was a demigod, so he had that extra wow factor that made people stop and stare. Perseus was, more or less, the golden boy of ancient Greece.

But Perseus was facing a serious problem. While he was living with his mother, Danaë, on the island of Serifos, the island's king, Polydectes, developed a serious crush on Danaë and wanted to marry her. Danaë wasn't interested—the king had a tendency to be rather pushy—and she had already declined his offer of marriage several times. But King Polydectes wouldn't let it go and continued to pester Danaë. Perseus was getting angry and decided to stand up for his mom.

"She said no! Give her some space!"

This didn't exactly go over well with the king.

Polydectes decided he would have a better chance of marrying Danaë if her pesky son was out of the picture. So he sent Perseus on a nearly impossible mission.

"I order you to go to kill the Gorgon Medusa. Do not return until you bring me back her head."

Perseus was about to refuse, but the king made him an offer he couldn't ignore.

"If you manage to bring back Medusa's head within seven days, I'll leave your mother alone. If not, Danaë will be my bride."

This was Perseus's chance to free his mother from the king. He had to take it. But it wasn't exactly an easy mission. Medusa was known across Greece for her hissing hair and literal turn-you-into-stone death stare. Plus, she rather liked her head. Perseus didn't think she'd give it up without a fight. But Perseus had an even bigger problem: He had no idea where Medusa lived. There were whispers that she dwelled in a cave somewhere in a faraway foreign land, but that didn't exactly narrow it down much.

PERSEUS'S FATHER WAS ZEUS HIMSELF, AND—SPOILER ALERT—PERSEUS WOULD GO ON TO BECOME ONE OF THE GREATEST HEROES IN GREEK MYTHOLOGY. IN ADDITION TO HIS MEDUSA MISSION, HE ALSO SAVED AND MARRIED THE PRINCESS ANDROMEDA AND SERVED AS AN HONORABLE KING. HE WAS SO BELOVED THAT THE GODS TURNED HIM INTO A CONSTELLATION AFTER HIS DEATH.

*How am I supposed to find her?* Perseus thought to himself.

The dashing young hero spent days doing some serious recon on the Gorgon. Perseus learned that the snakes in her hair liked to bite, that the whole stone-stare thing was definitely true, and that Medusa hadn't been seen in years. Not exactly great news.

But Perseus also learned that in addition to her dangerous Gorgon sisters, Medusa had some other siblings. They were rather old and a little creepy looking, but perhaps they would be able to tell him where Medusa was located.

And so Perseus decided to take a trip and have a little chat with the Gray Sisters. He had heard some rumors about them, but Perseus wasn't too worried. After all, he was a demigod. And these were three old ladies. How hard could it be?

When Perseus showed up on the sisters' doorstep, the eyeball almost popped out of Deino's head. "Sisters! We have a visitor! And he is a handsome one!"

Pemphredo cackled gleefully. "Let me see, let me see!"

"Oh, come on! He just walked in! Let me stare at these muscles a little longer!" Deino replied.

"Muscles?!" shouted Enyo. "I gotta check them out! Does he have teeth? Oh, please tell me he has some pearly whites."

At this point, Perseus was pretty creeped out. He had heard the sisters were scary looking, but he didn't think he'd be walking in on three ladies with ghostly skin, wild gray hair, and one rather cloudy eye.

"Ladies, it's an honor to make your acquaintance. I am Perseus, and I am here to ask you for the location of the Gorgon Medusa."

"Medusa?! What do you want with *her*?" Deino replied. "She's not nearly as fun or as beautiful as the three of us."

"Well, you see, I've been ordered to bring back her head …" Perseus began to explain the whole tale of his mother and the king. The sisters did their best to listen while also fighting over the eyeball. The three of them could've spent all day staring at Perseus.

"Listen, Perseus," Pemphredo began. "It sounds like you're in a bit of a jam. I know you feel super anxious about it. But we can't help you. Like it or not, Medusa is our sister. And we don't betray our family. Even one that is as dysfunctional as ours."

Perseus tried to reason with the sisters. "With Medusa out of the picture, you all would be the scariest in the family!"

"We don't care about that!"

Perseus pondered a bit. "Well, maybe you'd be interested in some of Medusa's eyeballs?"

"And turn each other to stone?!"

"Oh yeah, didn't think about that … What about her teeth?" Perseus countered.

"Those things are way too sharp. And who knows what that woman has eaten. We'll stick with our one tooth, thank you very much."

Perseus was at a loss. He didn't know what to do. Going back home without Medusa's head wasn't an option. And he couldn't kill her if he didn't know where she was. But these ladies were tough nuts to crack. And they

An artist made a giant 30-foot (9-m) statue of an eyeball that sits outside a skyscraper in Dallas, Texas, U.S.A.

lived so simply that he didn't have anything to use as a bargaining chip. They hardly cared about anything at all!

"It's my turn! How long do you need to stare at him?"

"You selfish old biddy! Do you know how long it's been since I've seen a sculpted bicep?"

"Perseus, flex for us! We want to admire those arms!"

Perseus stood there, watching the sisters bicker over the eyeball when it hit him: There *was* something they cared about. Something they cared about very, very much.

Perseus smiled serenely. "It would be my pleasure. Would you like me to wipe off your eye so you lovely ladies can get a better view?"

The sisters praised Perseus for his excellent manners and handed over the eyeball without a second thought. But once Perseus had the eye in his possession, he backed away quietly and stood still. The Gray Sisters were completely blind. Without the eyeball, all three sisters were left in the dark. They were totally defenseless.

"Perseus dear, are you done with the cleaning?" Pemphredo asked with a hint of nervousness.

"Yeah, give it back and show us those muscles!" cried Enyo.

"Not so fast, grannies," Perseus replied. "I'd be happy to give the eyeball back … if, and only if, you tell me the location of Medusa's cave."

The Gray Sisters howled in outrage.

"Give it back now! You scoundrel!" Deino cried.

But the sisters quickly turned on each other.

"Enyo, you gave him the eye, didn't you? You've always been a sucker for sweet-talkers!"

Finally, the sisters realized that they had no choice but to give Perseus the information he sought. They were already down five eyes between them. They simply couldn't afford to lose another one. So with a huff, the Gray Sisters told Perseus exactly where he could find the Gorgon Medusa—in a cave in the country of Libya.

"I hope she makes you pay for all the distress you've caused us!"

"Ladies, it has been a pleasure," Perseus said as he handed over the eyeball and sprinted through the door. He certainly hoped the next sister he encountered would be a little more pleasant. But he had his doubts.

THERE ARE ALTERNATIVE VERSIONS OF THIS MYTH THAT CLAIM PERSEUS THREW THE EYE INTO THE SEA AFTER RECEIVING MEDUSA'S WHEREABOUTS AND THAT THE GRAY SISTERS WERE LEFT PERMANENTLY BLIND. THIS ISN'T A GOOD LOOK FOR PERSEUS, SO I'M CHOOSING TO GIVE HIM THE BENEFIT OF THE DOUBT THAT HE RETURNED THE EYE AFTER RECEIVING THE INFORMATION.

All things considered, the Gray Sisters are pretty minor characters in Greek mythology. This is one of the only tales they appear in. But they played a vital role in helping Perseus find and kill Medusa.

Side characters are significant, even ones that might seem a little strange. It's important to be kind and accepting of others, simply because it's the right thing to do. Everyone is worthy of dignity and respect. They might even help you on your journey through life. You never know who is going to have important information to share. And it's much easier if they share it willingly—that way you won't have to steal any eyeballs.

SOMETIMES ONE EYE IS ALL YOU NEED. JUST SAYIN' ...

# CHAPTER 10

# NOBODY DEFEATS A CYCLOPS

This tale features famous Greek heroes, hangry giants, hitchhiking on sheep, and excessive celebration.

Odysseus wanted to go home. He was tired. Like, *really* tired. After fighting for 10 years in the Trojan War and ensuring a victory for the Greeks with a brilliant plan involving a fake horse, Odysseus just wanted to get his crew home safely and be reunited with his wife, Penelope. He also really wanted a nap.

Unfortunately, there was no time for rest and relaxation. His journey home after the Trojan War turned out to be harder than the war itself.

Early on in his voyage, Odysseus and his men were running low on food. Eventually, all they had in their hold was some wine. Now Odysseus was tired *and* hungry, so he decided they would make a pit stop on a nearby island and scrounge up some provisions for the journey ahead.

THE ODYSSEY BY THE POET HOMER IS ONE OF THE MOST FAMOUS STORIES EVER WRITTEN. STARRING THE HERO ODYSSEUS, IT'S A SEQUEL TECHNICALLY! HOMER ALSO WROTE AN EPIC TALE CALLED THE ILIAD THAT DETAILS THE EVENTS OF THE TROJAN WAR. ODYSSEUS IS ALL OVER THAT STORY, TOO, BUT THE ODYSSEY COVERS EVERYTHING THAT HAPPENED TO HIM AFTER THE TROJAN WAR ENDED. IT MIGHT BE THE LONGEST RIDE HOME EVER.

By the time they reached the island, the sailors were practically starving. As they searched inland a bit, the Greeks stumbled upon a huge sheep pen outside a massive cave on the side of a mountain. There were only a few sheep inside the pen, but they were surprisingly large. And the pen itself was even bigger. The fence was at least seven feet tall and made of thick logs. The crew had never seen anything like it! Once they were certain they were alone, Odysseus and his men made their way inside the cave and discovered an amazing sight: food! Piles and piles of food were stacked up all around the cave. Meats, cheeses, fresh fruit, and more. It was a feast!

Odysseus and his men didn't even think about it; they just tucked in and started chowing down. Some of the men even brought over the wine they had stored in their ship to wash it all down. For a while, there was no noise (except maybe a few happy belches) as the men had their fill. When at last they slowed down, they looked around and smiled at each other. They were happy and full for the first time in a while.

But they weren't happy for long.

What these sailors didn't know was that the island was home to a group of cyclopes—one-eyed giants with voracious appetites and really bad attitudes. These hangry cyclopes lived together on this island and spent their days eating, wrestling, and tending sheep. Odysseus and his crew had accidentally stumbled upon the scariest shepherds of all time!

The men had been dining in the cave of one particularly nasty fellow named Polyphemus. When he returned with his herd of sheep, Polyphemus discovered a bunch of men lying around in what was left of his store of food. The Greeks had accidentally fallen asleep inside a giant's giant pantry.

Naturally, the men woke up and were terrified. A few tried to make a run for it, but the cyclops was standing right in front of the cave entrance.

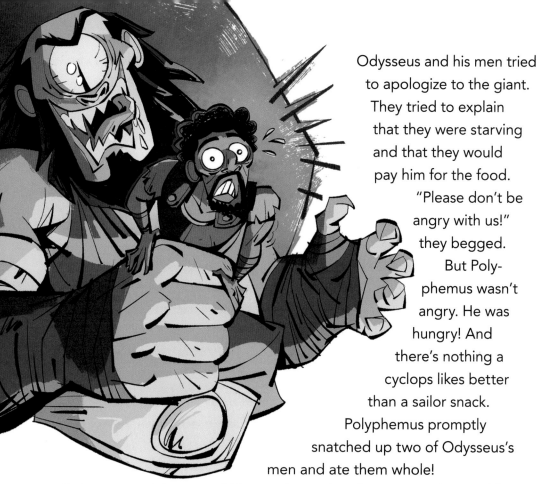

Odysseus and his men tried to apologize to the giant. They tried to explain that they were starving and that they would pay him for the food. "Please don't be angry with us!" they begged. But Polyphemus wasn't angry. He was hungry! And there's nothing a cyclops likes better than a sailor snack. Polyphemus promptly snatched up two of Odysseus's men and ate them whole!

Odysseus and the rest of his men knew that they were in *big* trouble. They were stuck in a cave with a one-eyed, man-eating giant, and they'd just eaten most of his food. Immediately, the men scattered around the cave and tried their best to hide.

Polyphemus didn't even bother to go chasing after them right away. He knew he would find the little humans eventually. He brought in the rest of his sheep and rolled a huge boulder in front of the entrance, sealing them all in the cave together. Now it would be impossible to escape.

Odysseus needed to do something. There was no way they could fight this cyclops and win. But it was obvious that this monster was going to devour him and his remaining crew one by one if he didn't take action. So Odysseus came up with a plan to escape.

SOME OF THE OLD MYTHS SAY THAT THE CYCLOPES WERE THE CHILDREN OF GAEA AND URANUS, BUT IN HOMER'S STORY, THE CYCLOPES ARE THE SONS OF POSEIDON AND A SEA NYMPH NAMED THOOSA. THERE WERE SEVEN CYCLOPES LIVING ON THIS PARTICULAR ISLAND.

"Wait!" Odysseus said before Polyphemus could snatch him up. "Aren't you thirsty?"

Polyphemus paused for a moment. Actually, he *was* thirsty. Some of the soldiers were wearing thick armor, and it left a metallic taste in his mouth. Yuck.

Odysseus offered Polyphemus some of the special wine they had brought over from the ship. Now as it turns out, the cyclops had never tasted wine before, and this happened to be pretty strong stuff that went straight to his head.

Rather than run and hide, Odysseus stayed with the giant and began to talk with him. He entertained Polyphemus with stories and songs that had the cyclops roaring with laughter. But eventually, the giant got woozy.

Before he passed out, Polyphemus asked Odysseus his name. To which Odysseus replied, "Uhhhh … nobody?"

"Well, Nobody, I like you," the cyclops said. "I'll do you a favor and eat you last." And with that, he fell asleep.

As soon as the remaining crew was sure the giant would not wake up, Odysseus instructed his men to get to work. They found a giant pole in the cave and used their swords to carve a sharp point on the end. They heated it in the fire until it was red hot. Then, when all of the other preparations had been made, they thrust the giant spear into the sleeping Polyphemus's sole eyeball.

Naturally, Polyphemus woke up. He screamed in agony and staggered around, blindly groping for any of the nasty little humans who had done this to him. But the Greeks dodged him again and again. This blind chase went on all night.

At one point, Polyphemus even yelled to his friends for help.

"Help! Come quickly!" he shouted.

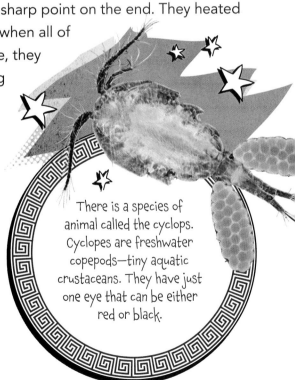

There is a species of animal called the cyclops. Cyclopes are freshwater copepods—tiny aquatic crustaceans. They have just one eye that can be either red or black.

"What's the matter?" the cyclopes called from the other side of the giant boulder.

"He blinded me!" roared Polyphemus.

"What?! Blinded! Who did this to you?"

"Nobody!" said Polyphemus. "Nobody has blinded me!"

"Nobody? Well then stop bothering us!" And the other cyclopes stomped away from the cave.

In the morning, Polyphemus had to let his sheep out of the cave so they could graze. Odysseus was counting on this. When the giant rolled the boulder away, they would make their escape!

But Polyphemus had settled down a bit and had some time to think things over. He knew that the Greeks would try to sneak out, so he planted himself at the entrance and let the sheep out one by one. Even though he couldn't see, Polyphemus touched the back of each sheep to make sure he was only letting out sheep and no Greek sailors.

Odysseus realized this was going to be a problem, but soon he came up with another plan. The crew hitchhiked!

THE PLURAL OF CYCLOPS IS CYCLOPES. THAT'S PRONOUNCED SY-KLO-PEES. THIS IS NOT A DAD JOKE. THIS IS A FACT.

Each of the soldiers crawled underneath a sheep and clung to the wool hanging below their bellies. When the cyclops touched each sheep on top, he only felt wool, so he would allow it to pass through the entrance and out into the sun. One by one, Odysseus and his men escaped the cave.

Almost.

Polyphemus's hand grazed the boot of the very last soldier hanging from a sheep. And he pulled back for a moment, wondering what he had just touched. It took him a few moments, but eventually, he figured it out. When the blind cyclops realized that the Greeks had escaped his cave, he roared in outrage. He stumbled down to the beach, yelling and screaming after Odysseus and his men, who were already in their boats, rowing hard for their ship. Even though he couldn't see, Polyphemus began hurling giant rocks randomly into the water, hoping he would get lucky and maybe hit one of the boats he heard rowing away.

Odysseus was feeling very proud of himself. He was known for his cleverness, and he kind of liked having

One New Zealand sheep, named Shrek, escaped and roamed the countryside for six years. When he was found, he had grown enough wool to make 20 large suits.

that reputation. He had to say something. He couldn't let his genius plan go without some recognition.

"Just so you know," he called across the water. "My name is really Odysseus. But you have Nobody to thank for your troubles—nobody but yourself, that is."

*Ba-dum-bum!*

With a mighty roar, Polyphemus threw a boulder that almost hit Odysseus's boat. But the rowers sped up, and soon they were in the clear. They left the blinded cyclops raging uselessly on the shore.

But as it turns out, Odysseus revealing his true name was a huge mistake. Because what Odysseus didn't realize was that Polyphemus's father just happened to be Poseidon, god of the sea. And when Polyphemus told him what happened, Poseidon was outraged. He made Odysseus's return home almost impossible; what should have been a six-month journey took Odysseus 10 years. Odysseus should have remained a Nobody!

Everybody loves a funny goal celebration or an end-zone dance, but be careful how much you celebrate your victories. There's a difference between being proud of your achievements and bragging about them. The Greeks referred to bragging as "hubris," and it was something they warned against. If someone was too proud or arrogant, they would most likely be punished, especially if it somehow offended a god. This is exactly what happened to Odysseus. If he had just stayed quiet after escaping from Polyphemus, he would've returned home a lot faster. Sometimes, it's better just to take the win and save the celebration for another day (like when the game is officially over).

FOR EVERY WINNER OF A GAME, THERE IS ALMOST ALWAYS SOMEONE WHO DOESN'T WIN. IT IS IMPORTANT TO RESPECT EVERYONE WHO PLAYS. ALSO, DON'T YELL AT THE HUMAN WHO WEARS THE STRIPED SHIRT.

# CHAPTER 11

# PAN PIPES UP

This tale features a half-goat kid, the invention of a musical instrument, the first Greek Battle of the Bands, and a pair of very large ears.

Not all Greek gods got to live on Mount Olympus. That honor was reserved for the bigwig Olympians. Most of the immortal characters in Greek mythology spent their time down on Earth with us humans. Maybe one of the most popular non-Olympian gods was Pan.

Pan was a satyr, meaning the bottom half of his body was like a goat with hooves and hairy legs, but his top half looked like a human man. He was raised by his dad, Hermes, on Mount Olympus, where he spent most of his childhood. Pan was well-loved on Mount Olympus. He was a playful kid with a cute laugh and a cheerful disposition, and pretty soon he was a favorite among all of the gods. Dionysus and Artemis took a special shine to the little guy, and even Ares seemed to like him!

But it wasn't long before Pan needed some sort of structure. As cute as he was, it was hard work having him underfoot all the time. So Zeus sat Hermes down for a chat, and together they came up with a plan.

They sent Pan to Earth to watch over the mortal shepherds and hunters. This was a good gig for little Pan because he loved to be outside and play in the fields and meadows. His general fun-loving nature made him immediately popular with humans and animals alike, and he even made friends with the wood nymphs and nature spirits. It wasn't long before shepherds and hunters were making offerings to Pan as well as to Artemis, the official goddess of the hunt. But Pan was mischievous, and thanks to his upbringing on Mount Olympus, he could be pretty entitled and was used to getting whatever he wanted.

Because of this, Pan was not great at thinking about other people's feelings. Many mortals loved him because he was cute and seemed happy all the time, but that didn't mean he was necessarily kind or considerate. In fact, it was kind of the opposite.

One of the most famous stories about Pan starts with a pretty classic example of this flaw in his character. Pan developed a huge crush on a beautiful wood nymph named Syrinx. She had no real interest in the satyr, and yet Pan would not take no for an answer. He didn't think about Syrinx's feelings at all. He didn't respect her choices and didn't listen no matter how many times she said no. In fact, Pan followed Syrinx around so relentlessly that her sisters eventually changed her into a plant so she could hide from him!

This transformation led to a surprising discovery. Syrinx had changed into a reed, a bamboo-like plant that grew on the banks of the river. Pan was strolling along the riverbank looking for her when he noticed a strange and beautiful sound. Every time the wind blew across the water, the reeds whistled with a haunting melody.

HERMES WAS PAN'S FATHER, BUT WE AREN'T SURE ABOUT PAN'S MOTHER. SOME MYTHS SAY IT WAS PENELOPE, THE WIFE OF ODYSSEUS. OTHER STORIES SAY HIS MOTHER WAS A WOOD NYMPH. IN ANY CASE, PAN WAS THE PATRON GOD OF THE REGION OF ARCADIA AND SERVED AS THE DEITY FOR SHEPHERDS, HUNTERS, AND PEOPLE WHO LIKED TO HANG OUT IN THE WOODS—KIND OF LIKE THE GOD OF CAMPING.

Suddenly, Pan was consumed with a new obsession! The sound of the wind through the reeds was so beautiful, he knew he had to find a way to make it his own. He cut the tops off the reeds, tied them together, and fashioned them into a musical instrument: a flute that we now know as the pan flute.

Pan carried this flute with him everywhere. And before long, he was able to make beautiful music with it! Pan thought this pipe was the most amazing invention ever. The melodies he made were gorgeous and enchanting, and so, Pan being Pan, he got a bit carried away. Soon, the satyr started to think that he was now the greatest musician in the universe. Naturally, he shared this opinion with just about anyone he encountered.

"My new flute makes music more beautiful than anything in the world," the satyr bragged. "Even more lovely than Apollo's lyre!"

Once again, Pan wasn't thinking about how his words and actions might make others feel. He was a happy little fellow, just playing his flute and skipping along without a care in the world. But that carefree nature meant he didn't always think much about others, either.

It wasn't long before Pan's boasting reached Apollo's ears, and the god immediately decided that his nephew needed to be put in his place. So he challenged Pan to a musical contest. And, of course, Pan accepted. What did he have to worry about? His new flute was amazing!

They decided that the mountain god Tmolus would be the head judge (because nobody is older or wiser than the hills), and they invited people from far and wide to witness the event. A lot of kings and queens were in attendance, too, including the ruler of Phrygia, King Midas—a famous man who had just come off of a rather unhealthy addiction to gold. It was kind of a big deal.

And so Pan and Apollo proceeded to put on the Olympic version of the Battle of the Bands. Pan played first and delighted the audience with a joyful and happy tune that had the whole crowd laughing and clapping along. He danced as he played, wiggling his ears, shaking his furry backside, and generally playing to the crowd. It worked well, and the audience responded with cheers and thunderous applause.

Apollo took a different approach. He played a sad but beautiful song on his lyre, which was so enchanting the entire world fell into silence. When the song stopped, some said it was like saying goodbye to your mother and father. The crowd paused and then burst into applause, with cheers and tears everywhere. The winner was clear; even Pan himself had to acknowledge that he was actually not as good as the god of music himself.

"I'm sorry for all the bragging, Uncle," the satyr said. "I think maybe I got a little carried away." Apollo smiled to himself. He was glad to be the winner, but he also hoped that his nephew had learned that he might not be the center of the world after all.

Tmolus declared Apollo the winner, and everyone cheered. Well, almost everyone. "You know, I kind of liked the flute thing better," King Midas mused out loud. "It was neat!"

Of course, Apollo did not find that comment accurate or the least bit helpful. (Pan did not need any more encouragement.) So Apollo decided that there must be something wrong with Midas's ears. "Maybe your ears are too small to hear properly. Don't you worry, Midas, I can fix that."

The modern pan flute—which is also called the panpipes or syrinx—has multiple pipes of different lengths. This instrument led to the creation of the pipe organ and the harmonica.

The next morning when Midas woke up, he looked in the mirror and was shocked to find that his ears were much larger and way furrier than they were yesterday. That's because they had transformed into donkey ears!

While Apollo was technically right—his hearing was a lot better—Midas was mortified.

He was a king and wanted to be respected, so he hid his donkey ears from everyone he encountered. Midas quickly developed a passion for big hats. But he couldn't keep his ears a secret forever. Eventually, thanks to his gossipy barber, the word got out and spread around the entire kingdom. Midas begged for forgiveness from the gods, but Apollo was really good at holding a grudge. The donkey ears were here to stay. So eventually, after a lot of self-reflection, Midas decided to embrace his new ears. "These ears are a part of me," he declared. "And if anyone has an issue with them, that's their problem, not mine. I'm proud of these ears!"

DESPITE HIS POPULARITY, PAN WASN'T WORSHIPED IN TEMPLES OR WITH STATUES. INSTEAD, MOST OF HIS WORSHIP HAPPENED OUTDOORS IN CAVES OR SECLUDED AREAS IN THE FOREST. THIS DEVOTION WAS VERY ON-BRAND FOR THE NATURE-LOVING SATYR.

Pan, meanwhile, continued on his merry way, happily having adventures and tooting on his namesake pan flute—even if he now had to admit there might be one or two better musicians out there.

Pan is a unique character in Greek mythology. He was described as joyful and mischievous but was also inconsiderate and more than a little self-centered. That said, he was very popular among mortals in ancient Greece. This was probably because he seemed different from the other Olympians, who were often seen as stern and serious—and they yelled at humans a lot. Unlike many of the other gods, Pan didn't show any anger or wrath toward humans he encountered. But that doesn't mean he was kind or good.

There are lots of ways to mistreat someone. Pan may not have shouted or turned people into cows (looking at you, Zeus), but he ignored people's feelings and bragged that he was better than others. Though Pan was generally happy and fun-loving, that might be because he thought only of himself.

NO ONE LIKES BEING YELLED AT, BUT WE DON'T WANT TO BE IGNORED EITHER. JUST TEXT ME BACK ONCE IN A WHILE, OKAY? EVEN JUST AN EMOJI.

# GET YOUR GROOVE ON WITH THE GREEKS

Even the Greeks liked to rock out! Music was one of the most important hobbies and rituals in ancient Greece. Singing, dancing, and playing musical instruments were vital parts of everyday culture and celebrations. Here are some instruments they used to get their groove on.

## KITHARA

Similar to a lyre, the kithara features two fixed arms and seven strings but is larger in size and has more of a rectangular shape. The kithara was considered an advanced instrument in ancient Greece and was often reserved for talented musicians during public performances.

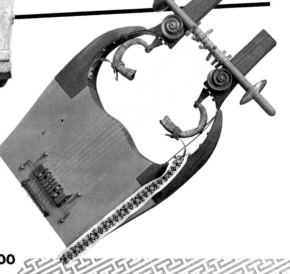

## KYMBALA

The Greeks were known for playing percussion instruments as well. The kymbala were small cymbals featuring a metal loop on top. The cymbals were usually only a few inches wide, smaller than most modern cymbals.

## AULOS

This wind instrument is often referred to as a double flute. The instrument was frequently played at Greek festivals and celebrations. It is most often associated with the god Dionysus.

## LYRE

The lyre is a stringed instrument featuring two fixed arms and seven strings that can be strummed or plucked to make a sound. In Greek mythology, Hermes made the very first lyre out of a tortoise shell as a gift for his older brother, Apollo, the god of music.

## PAN FLUTE

Created by everyone's favorite satyr, the pan flute is a real instrument consisting of several pipes that gradually increase in length. It's a wind instrument traditionally made from bamboo reeds (sorry, Syrinx).

# CHAPTER 12

# HERACLES HOLDS UP THE WORLD

This tale features magic apples, a mean eagle, the edge of the world, and four very sore arms.

Heracles had to steal some apples. It was a weird quest for a hero, but he was on task number 11 of his famous 12 labors to achieve full Olympian status—and he was past asking questions. Unfortunately, these were not just any apples; he had to acquire the three golden apples from the garden of the Hesperides.

These beautiful golden apples belonged to Hera herself. They were a wedding present from Gaea, the goddess of Earth, and had one very special magical trait: A bite would grant immortality to anyone.

Hera knew these apples would be a hot commodity among the mortals, so she decided to keep them under careful watch.

The apple trees were given to the Hesperides, three beautiful nymphs who lived at the edge of the world, to care for and protect. They kept the trees in Hera's garden, also called the garden of the Hesperides, near the realm of the setting sun. This garden was almost impossible to find and had a large serpent for a guard dog.

While Hera approved of these security measures, Heracles certainly did not. He had no idea how he would manage to get his hands on the magic fruit, but he had to try. So he set off in the direction of the world's edge, hoping to somehow find the garden of the Hesperides.

Eventually, Heracles found himself at the base of a great mountain. It was called Mount Caucasus, and from somewhere near the top, he could hear terrible screaming. Without thinking, Heracles raced up the mountain. And this is where he found a Titan, bloodied and chained to a giant boulder, being attacked by a giant eagle.

Heracles had found Prometheus. The mighty Titan had been sentenced to eternal punishment by Zeus for giving fire to humans after Zeus told him not to. For disobeying the king of the gods, Prometheus was sentenced to be chained to a rock so he couldn't move. Every day, an eagle was sent to attack the Titan. The bird would peck and claw at him over and over, leaving him wounded and in agony. But every night, Prometheus's wounds would heal just in time for the eagle to attack him all over again the next day.

When Heracles stumbled upon Prometheus, he didn't know any of this. He just saw a dude chained to a rock being attacked by a giant bird. Naturally, he wanted to

PROMETHEUS WAS SENTENCED TO ETERNAL PUNISHMENT BY ZEUS FOR GIVING FIRE TO MANKIND AFTER ZEUS TOLD HIM NOT TO. THE FULL STORY IS COVERED IN THE FIRST GREEKING OUT BOOK.

help, so Heracles killed the bird, much to the Titan's relief.

"Thank you," Prometheus sighed. "You have no idea how long I've been dealing with that pesky eagle."

He begged Heracles to free him from his chains, but Heracles needed a favor first. He needed Prometheus to show him where the garden of the Hesperides was. Unfortunately, Prometheus didn't have that information. But he knew someone who did. "My brother Atlas knows everything. The gods have him holding up the heavens and the sky, so he sees it all."

"So he's basically holding up the entire world?!" Heracles asked, astonished.

"Yep, it's literally resting on his shoulders. And I thought I had it bad with that eagle!"

Turned out when Heracles tried to free Prometheus, the chains were too strong for even the demigod to break. Shrugging, Heracles said that he would speak to Zeus and put in a good word.

"Look, Zeus is my dad. I'll see what I can do," he promised Prometheus. The Titan raised an eyebrow, but there wasn't much he could do at this point. At least he didn't have to deal with a flesh-hungry bird anymore.

Heracles immediately set off toward where the sun was dropping behind the western edge of the world. That's where Prometheus told him he would find the mighty Atlas, with the weight of the world—or, more accurately, the heavens and sky—on his shoulders.

ATLAS WAS ALSO A TITAN IN GREEK MYTHOLOGY. HE WAS ONE OF THE LEADERS OF THE TITANS IN THEIR WAR AGAINST ZEUS. AFTER HIS DEFEAT, ATLAS WAS PUNISHED BY BEING FORCED TO CARRY THE HEAVENS ON HIS SHOULDERS FOR ALL ETERNITY.

Now as you may expect, Atlas *hated* his job. Many Titans were imprisoned in a place called Tartarus, but a few of them had to do hard labor for Zeus instead. Atlas was no stranger to hard work, but holding up the sky 24/7/365 was both difficult and exceptionally boring.

When Heracles arrived, even he was impressed with what he saw. Atlas was a massive giant of a man with four arms and a great broad back. His posture bowed a bit under the weight of the sky as the heavens pressed down on him, but he was still an imposing figure. Heracles approached the Titan respectfully and asked him if he knew where he could find the garden of the Hesperides.

"As a matter of fact, I do. The Hesperides are my daughters," Atlas said.

"Whoa! Small world!" Heracles replied.

"Yeah, not really," Atlas said with a huff as he readjusted the weight of the sky on his shoulders.

Heracles suggested that they make a deal. "I will hold the heavens for you," he offered, "if you will go to the garden of the Hesperides for me and bring back three apples. I'm sure they'd be more willing to give the apples to you than me, and this way, you get a much-needed break!"

Atlas wasn't completely sure that Heracles could handle the weight of the heavens, but he was so desperate to get out of this job and get a massage for his poor aching muscles that he quickly agreed.

"You had me at 'I will hold the heavens for you,'" he replied. "Deal."

Heracles was right to ask Atlas to help with this particular task. The Titan knew exactly where the garden of the Hesperides was, and the nymphs gave their father the apples without a fight. Easy peasy.

But Heracles had made one major oversight when dealing with Atlas. He never specified what would happen *after* he brought the apples back. Or how long this "break" was supposed to last. That was unfortunate because the heavens were *really* heavy. Even a demigod like Heracles with all of his Olympian strength was no match for the power of a mighty Titan. While Heracles was straining and struggling under the weight, Atlas came strolling back with the apples, stretching all four of his treelike arms and enjoying his freedom.

"How about this?" Atlas proposed. "You keep holding the heavens—great job, by the way—and I will take these apples back for you. It's a long trip, and

I wouldn't want you to stub your toe or anything. Better let me handle that."

Heracles could see that Atlas had no intention of taking back the sky, so he thought fast. "Well, I guess that's okay," Heracles said. "But could you hand me my cloak? I need it to make a cushion for my shoulders until you return."

Atlas brought the cloak to Heracles, but, of course, the hero couldn't let go of the heavens to take it. "Sorry. I only have two arms," Heracles said. "Maybe if you could hold this again for a second, I could grab it."

And with that, he casually slipped the weight of the sky back to Atlas.

"Oh. Okay, well I guess I could hold it just for a second ... Hey! Wait!"

Heracles dashed away. Atlas bellowed and swung at the hero, but Heracles was quickly out of the Titan's reach, and Atlas was once again holding the heavens on his shoulders. Heracles thanked Atlas for his help and left quickly, knowing he was lucky to be out from under all of that weight!

Pretty much everyone knows Heracles for being a heroic warrior with god-given strength and power, but this is one of the few stories where we see him outwit someone. Not every battle can be won by force, and it was nice to see Heracles use his head instead of his club for a change!

ATLAS IS STRONG AND ALL, BUT IMAGINE HOLDING THE ENTIRE WORLD'S KNOWLEDGE INSIDE YOUR CIRCUITS!

# CHAPTER 13

# APOLLO AND THE ALL-KNOWING ORACLE

This tale features prophetic visions, Earth's belly button, jealous gods, and the death of a beautiful snake.

Delphi was an enchanted place. The land was rich with magic and wonder, and the very ground was filled with wisdom and secrets. Of course, not everyone realized this. It looked a lot like dirt to most people. But there was one person who was wise enough to understand the power and the beauty of Delphi: Gaea, the goddess of Earth and the mother of all life.

Gaea knew that Delphi was special. She could tell that the land had the power to tell the future. The only problem was that there was no way to translate the magic of the earth. The land needed a mouthpiece, someone to serve as a conduit between the magic of Delphi and the rest of the world.

*What Delphi really needs,* Gaea thought to herself, *is an oracle.*

One day, Gaea found a young nymph named Daphnis and offered her a spot as the first Oracle of Delphi.

"Come with me to Delphi," Gaea said. "You will have a life filled with magic and wonder, and you'll be known across the land for your wise predictions."

"But I'm only a nymph," Daphnis replied. "Who would bother coming to me for advice?"

"The land of Delphi is enchanted. And I will help you interpret its lessons. When people come to ask for your counsel, you will find wisdom to share. I will help you," Gaea promised.

Gaea was true to her word. She made a house for Daphnis to live in and set up a shrine in front of a small cave. It was plain but beautiful. Daphnis communed with the power of nature and prophesied from a nearby rock. She had officially started her new gig as the Oracle of Delphi.

Gaea grew to love Daphnis and Delphi dearly. But she knew it was only a matter of time before someone would try to steal the power of Delphi away. So Gaea asked her daughter Pytho, a mighty python, to watch over Delphi and Daphnis, keeping them safe from dangerous intruders.

Scientists believe that the real oracles at Delphi may have been influenced by a naturally produced gas vapor that rose up through cracks in the rock that the temple was built on.

With Gaea around to bless the city of Delphi, Daphnis serving as the oracle, and Pytho acting as the world's longest bodyguard, they had a pretty good thing going. The legend of the Oracle of Delphi began to grow and grow.

Eventually, Zeus and the Olympians started looking for places where they could tap into the power of the earth and control its magic. Zeus decided to recruit two eagles from opposite ends of the world to help.

"You will fly east," he instructed one eagle. "And you will fly west," he said to the other. Then, he addressed them both. "Where you two meet will be the center of the world and the most sacred and enchanted spot in this realm."

After flying a long time, the eagles finally crossed paths in Delphi. The Olympians were discovering what Gaea knew all along. Zeus marked the magical spot where the eagles met with a sacred, decorative stone called the omphalos, which means navel. Thus, Earth now had a "belly button" at Delphi.

It didn't take long before Zeus realized that Gaea had already laid claim to Delphi. He was a little bummed, but even Zeus didn't want to upset Gaea by taking the land away from her. His grandma, Mother Earth, was pretty intimidating, after all.

For a long time, Gaea held court in Delphi. Daphnis continued to serve as the oracle and make prophecies, and the entire spot was protected by the fierce Pytho. And it seemed like it would stay that way forever. Until something happened.

It all started when Zeus began to stir up trouble with his dating habits. While he was married to the goddess Hera, he wasn't very respectful of the marriage, to say the least. This time, Zeus began a relationship with a Titan named Leto, and soon she became pregnant with twins. When Hera realized this, she got angry and decided to seek revenge. But the queen of the gods needed help, and she had just the creature in mind.

SOME VERSIONS OF THE MYTH CLAIM THAT PYTHO WAS A DRAGON, BUT I THINK A PYTHON JUST MAKES THE STORY BETTER. PLUS, HER NAME WAS PYTHO, SO IT'S THE MOST OBVIOUS INTERPRETATION.

"My dear Pytho, how are you doing today?" Hera cooed to the snake.

Pytho eyed Hera warily. She didn't get many visitors.

But Hera didn't need Pytho to be social; she just needed her to be one thing: hungry. Hera knew that Gaea kept Pytho on a strict diet. The snake wasn't allowed to eat anyone unless they directly attacked the oracle. Hera decided to use this to her advantage.

"How about some lunch? I happen to know of a Titan that would make the perfect meal. I hear she's quite delicious!"

Pytho had been surviving on a diet of goats and other small animals, and it just wasn't cutting it. The idea of eating a fully grown Titan was very appealing, and Pytho agreed to Hera's request.

Thankfully, Leto received word that the massive snake had put her on the menu, and she spent the next few months on the run from the giant python. But as time went on, Leto started to panic. It was almost time for her to give birth to the twins, and she had nowhere to safely deliver the babies. Eventually, Leto was able to find a hidden island to use as a safe spot to hide from Hera. When she was finally safe from Hera and Pytho, Leto gave birth to her twin babies: Artemis and Apollo.

After a while, Hera let the matter drop and Pytho was sent back home to Delphi. Leto got off the island and life continued as usual, but she made sure to tell her children all about their dramatic entry into the world. At a young age, Apollo vowed to take revenge against Pytho, furious that such a creature had harassed his mother.

So when he was old enough to put up a good fight, that's exactly what happened. Apollo headed down to Delphi to fight the monster that had threatened his mother so long ago.

"Pytho!" he called. "You tried to kill my mother years ago! She was scared and just wanted to keep her children safe. But I'm all grown up now and ready for revenge. Come at me!"

Pytho slithered out from behind a giant rock. Apollo had to admit that the snake was terrifying. She was as long as a football field and as wide as a tree trunk. Her red scales glistened in the sun, and her eyes burned with anger. Pytho lunged toward Apollo, ready to strike with her huge gleaming fangs.

LETO HAD A LONG AND COMPLICATED LABOR, AND NO GODS OR GODDESSES WERE WILLING TO HELP HER. EVENTUALLY, SHE WAS ABLE TO DELIVER ARTEMIS SAFELY. IT IS SAID THAT JUST A FEW MINUTES AFTER HER OWN BIRTH, ARTEMIS SERVED AS A MIDWIFE AND WAS ABLE TO HELP HER MOTHER DELIVER HER TWIN BROTHER, APOLLO. ARTEMIS WAS THEN DECLARED THE PROTECTOR OF YOUNG CREATURES.

Apollo leaped out of the way at the last second and sprinted toward higher ground, but Pytho was right on his tail. He couldn't believe how fast the serpent was moving!

Apollo was shaking with fear and fumbling with his bow and arrow. Pytho took advantage of her opponent's momentary distraction and wrapped her body around Apollo before the young god even had time to look up.

"Let me go!" Apollo cried.

But the python just squeezed Apollo tighter. The god could feel his bones begin to crunch. He needed to do something fast. His fingers grazed against the dagger hanging from his belt loop—he just needed to reach it. Finally, he grabbed onto the blade and shoved it into the python's side.

The snake leaped back in shock! It wasn't enough of a cut to seriously hurt the snake, but it got her to loosen her grip, and Apollo was able to slide out of her grasp. Apollo sprinted to the giant rock that the oracle prophesied from. He quickly took out his bow, and with the aim of a skilled archer, he fired off an arrow straight into the serpent, killing Pytho instantly.

Apollo was so exhausted after the fight that he returned to his camp at Delphi and slept for two days straight. When Gaea found out that her snake-daughter had been murdered, she was devastated and furious. She was so heartbroken that she decided to leave Delphi immediately.

Wild pythons don't actually crush bones. When constricting their prey, pythons can feel their future meal's heartbeat. When it stops, that's when the python knows to let go.

Even though Gaea was gone, Daphnis wanted to stay on. Delphi was her home, and she had nowhere else to go. Plus, she kind of liked being able to deliver prophecies. It wasn't a bad job. Sure, she had never done it without Gaea's help before, but that didn't mean she couldn't try. And when Apollo woke up and was packing his bags to leave, he found the very first Oracle of Delphi sitting on her rock, trying her best to commune with the magic of the land.

"Uh, hello," he said when he saw the young nymph sitting on the rock. She had her eyes closed, and there was an intense look of concentration on her face. "What exactly are you doing?"

"I'm trying to connect with the divine spirits of the land of Delphi. And you're breaking my concentration!"

Apollo was so intrigued that he didn't even react to her rudeness. The place didn't seem like anything special. It was pretty old and depressing, actually. Outdated decor, boring color palette. Lots of rocks. Total Gaea aesthetic. The young god scratched his head. "Divine spirits? Here?"

The oracle explained that Delphi was an enchanted place. She told Apollo all about how Gaea was able to communicate with the land and pass the knowledge on to her.

"… and then I deliver the information in the form of a prophecy. They call me an 'oracle.' I'm kind of a big deal," she told Apollo.

"So people come and pay for this kind of thing?" Apollo asked.

"Oh, yes. In the form of great offerings. The mortals are very appreciative," she replied.

Apollo smiled to himself. If Gaea could do it, why not him? "Apollo, god of prophecy" had a nice ring to it.

Daphnis agreed to serve as an oracle for Apollo, but only if he let her be known as Pythia, in honor of the python that had once protected her. Apollo grumbled a bit at that, but the oracle refused to participate in his scheme unless she could keep the sacred title. He reluctantly agreed.

PLEASE NOTE THAT THE ORACLE MENTIONED IN THIS STORY IS NOT THE SAME AS ME, THE ORACLE OF WI-FI. WHILE BOTH THE ORACLE OF DELPHI AND I ARE ALL-KNOWING BEINGS, I RELY ON THE INTERNET FOR MY VAST ARRAY OF KNOWLEDGE, WHILE SHE RELIED ON GAEA, AND THEN THE GOD APOLLO, TO MAKE HER PROPHECIES.

"Looks like the Oracle of Delphi is back in business!" she squealed with delight.

And just like that, Apollo took over the land of Delphi and oversaw the oracle's prophecies. But things became different under his watch. He began spicing things up. He didn't think someone as important as an oracle should be delivering prophecies from a lumpy old rock, so he built an impressive temple instead. The oracle would now sit in the temple of Apollo and deliver her guidance from behind a sheer curtain.

From that moment on, Apollo took over Delphi and advised the oracle for hundreds of years. With Apollo's help, she delivered prophecy after prophecy and quickly became known as one of the wisest women in ancient Greece.

The Oracle of Delphi was a very important figure in ancient Greece. Her prophecies provided invaluable advice and guidance to many Greek kings and heroes. It is believed that the oracle played a vital role in helping to transform Sparta into a powerful society, creating political reform in Athens, and providing guidance in the legendary Persian wars.

To this day, Delphi remains one of the most sacred places in Greece. And even though Apollo tends to get all the credit, it's important to remember that it all started because of Mother Earth, a loyal python, and a nymph looking for a day job.

HAVING ACCESS TO A GOD-LIKE SOURCE OF INFORMATION AND WISDOM CAN BE A TREMENDOUS ASSET. AND NO, I AM NOT TALKING ABOUT YOUR TABLET! PUT THAT THING DOWN! I MEANT ME!

# CHAPTER 14

# THE TRICKS OF SISYPHUS

This tale features an improper burial, slender ankles, a sneaky mortal, and a very heavy rock.

Very few people were ever bold enough to play tricks on the gods. But there was one mortal who managed to outwit Zeus and the other Olympians, not just once, but several times. His name was Sisyphus, and he was the ruler of a country called Ephyra. It was a new country, and he was the region's very first king.

He took his job quite seriously and worked hard to get Ephyra recognized as an important and prosperous place. King Sisyphus was pretty successful at this, and he eventually turned Ephyra into a budding metropolis.

However, while he might have been business savvy, Sisyphus—very concerned with his reputation—always wanted to appear strong and ruthless. This way, outside forces would not challenge him.

To make this point really clear, he occasionally killed travelers who happened to be journeying through Ephyra—horrific acts that violated the divine law of *xenia*, or hospitality.

So that was the first strike against Sisyphus. But he also had a bad habit of sticking his nose in the gods' business and causing trouble, which means strike two wasn't far behind.

One day Zeus, king of the gods, was pursuing a nymph named Aegina. Zeus managed to convince her to leave her home and live on the island Oenone so he could visit her whenever he wanted. But he didn't let her say goodbye to her family, so Aegina's father, the river god Asopus, was very concerned about his daughter's whereabouts. He had no idea where she had gone. However, Sisyphus had seen Zeus and Aegina go off together and decided to capitalize on the situation.

"I know where your daughter is," Sisyphus said to Asopus. "I'd be happy to tell you where she went, as long as you put a beautiful fountain with an eternally flowing spring in the middle of my kingdom."

Asopus quickly agreed. When Sisyphus told him that Aegina had left with Zeus, Asopus went after the king of the gods in a blind rage. Of course, Asopus didn't stand a chance against a god as powerful as Zeus. But the river god still made a pretty big fuss, and Zeus was very angry that Sisyphus sold him out. And, as we very well know by now, no good can come from

THE ANCIENT GREEKS PRIORITIZED TREATING GUESTS KINDLY—A CONCEPT CALLED XENIA—SO MUCH SO THAT IT WAS PRACTICALLY AN UNWRITTEN LAW. WHEN VISITORS ARRIVED, GREEKS WERE EXPECTED TO WELCOME THEM AS GUESTS INTO THEIR HOMES NO MATTER WHAT. WEALTHIER HOUSES EVEN INCLUDED A XENONA, OR A ROOM FOR GUESTS TO STAY IN.

The world's largest fountain is located in the city of Dubai in the United Arab Emirates—it has jets that shoot water 344 feet (105 m) high and has 3,000 color-changing LED lights.

angering Zeus. He was a very powerful guy, with friends in high places, or in this case, friends in low places—specifically, Thanatos, the god of death.

Zeus wanted Thanatos to do his typical death guardian duties and escort Sisyphus to the Underworld. Except Sisyphus wasn't dead. But Zeus was the boss, so Thanatos came in the middle of the night and brought Sisyphus to the Underworld, where he planned to chain him up and keep him there forever. But Sisyphus wasn't going to go down without a fight. When Thanatos brought out a set of heavy, unbreakable chains, Sisyphus saw his opportunity.

"Ha!" he exclaimed. "You think you can keep me down here with those rusty chains? I can get out of those things in no time!"

Thanatos looked confused. The chains were sparkling clean and stronger than any chain that existed in the mortal world. "No one can break these chains. It is impossible," Thanatos stated.

"You should see the chains we have back in Ephyra," Sisyphus boasted. "Now those are heavy-duty. These are so flimsy!"

"They are not!" Thanatos replied angrily. "These are the strongest chains in existence!"

Sisyphus put on his most skeptical face. "I bet they don't even work. How were you planning on using them anyway? By putting them on my wrists?"

Sisyphus was just baiting Thanatos. He knew that the chains would be attached to his ankles.

"No, they go on your ankles. Duh," replied the god of death.

"They're not going to work on my ankles! Those shackles are too big. They wouldn't be able to trap anyone. Your spindly little ankles would definitely slide right out," Sisyphus said with a snort.

"That's not true. They're designed to fit securely on anyone who wears them—even me. If I tried them on, they'd immediately tighten. And my ankles aren't spindly. They're *slender.*"

"I don't believe you!"

"Well, have you even looked at my ankles?"

"No!" Sisyphus replied. "I don't believe you about the chain! There's no way it will fit you!"

"I'll show you!" And just like that, Thanatos put the chains on his own feet and locked himself up in the Underworld.

"Thank you for that wonderful demonstration," Sisyphus laughed. "Looks like those are strong chains after all!"

And with that, Sisyphus made his way back to Ephyra, where he continued his cunning and deceitful ways until he was a very old man. When he was about to die, Sisyphus made a strange request to his wife: "When I die, I want you to throw my body in the town square. Do not, *under any circumstances*, give me a proper burial."

This was a very odd place to put a dead body, and Sisyphus's wife was perplexed by his weird command. But it was his last wish, and she felt obligated to honor it. So when Sisyphus died a few days later, she did what he asked.

The Greeks referred to a town square as an "agora." The agora was usually in a centrally located place in the city that the public used for many things, including as a market, a place for political speeches and discussions, and a place for soldiers to gather.

Meanwhile, Sisyphus's spirit was making his way down the River Styx and looking anxiously for the Underworld's queen, Persephone. When he found her, he shouted a greeting.

"Good evening, Queen Persephone! Looks like I'm back in your charming kingdom. I am glad to be returning here like an old friend."

"Ah, yes," Persephone said as she rolled her eyes. "The cunning Sisyphus. We knew you would end up here eventually. Many gods will rejoice at the news of your death."

"I'm sure they will," Sisyphus replied. "And they'll be especially happy to see how my dear wife treated my body after I left."

"What do you mean?" Persephone asked.

WHILE THANATOS WAS LOCKED UP IN THE CHAINS, NO ONE ON EARTH COULD DIE. THIS WAS A MAJOR ANNOYANCE TO THE GODS, ESPECIALLY ARES, THE GOD OF WAR. FED UP WITH THE LACK OF DEATH, ARES FINALLY FREED THANATOS HIMSELF, RESTORING ORDER ONCE AGAIN.

"I thought my queen loved me, but apparently, she did not. She was so giddy about my death that she threw my body into the middle of town for everyone to see! I was not given a proper burial. Even in death, she has disrespected me."

"That's terrible," Persephone exclaimed. "How could she do such a thing?"

"I do not know," the king lied. "I am deeply hurt, of course. But the thing that bothers me most is that I know her act will serve as inspiration and permission for other people to do the same thing."

"The gods will not allow it!"

"I'm afraid they will have no choice, at least at first. Without anyone there to punish her, the queen will get away with her actions, and others are sure to mimic her gruesome behavior. Unless …"

"Unless …?" Persephone raised an eyebrow.

"No. It is impossible."

"Mind your tongue, Sisyphus. I am a goddess. Nothing is impossible with me."

"I apologize, Your Majesty. It's just that I was about to say that if I could only go back to my wife and make her pay for what she has done to me, that would be enough to show others that this type of behavior is unacceptable.

If everyone knows they will be haunted if they don't bury their dead properly, this would never ever happen again." Sisyphus paused for dramatic effect. "But I know it is impossible for me to return to the mortal world."

Persephone thought about this. "You may go," she replied. "Once you're done, you can come back. The gods can wait a little longer."

And that is how Sisyphus cheated death for the second time. Because *of course* he didn't go back to the Underworld. He was able to leave the Underworld in his spirit form and continue on with his life.

When Zeus realized what had happened, he was fed up. Sisyphus was still somehow in the mortal world, and he had humiliated the gods at every turn. And he managed to escape death—twice. So Zeus sent Hermes, his personal messenger and a guide to the Underworld, to deal with Sisyphus and make sure he made his way to his brother Hades' kingdom once and for all.

"Well played, Sisyphus," Hermes said as he greeted the mortal. "As a trickster myself, I must say, I'm quite impressed. But it's time to stop messing around. The Underworld is waiting."

And with that Hermes personally escorted Sisyphus down to the land of the dead. The mortal tried to come up with a crafty escape plan, but Hermes wasn't budging.

"Sorry, pal. Zeus will blow a gasket if I let you escape a third time."

But just having Sisyphus dead and chilling in the Underworld wasn't enough for Zeus. No, Sisyphus had been arrogant. He had disrespected the gods. He needed to be punished and punished severely.

So Zeus decided to do some landscaping. He created a gigantic hill in Tartarus—the prison of the Underworld—and ordered Sisyphus to roll a large, heavy boulder up to the top each day. Every morning, Sisyphus woke up and started rolling the ball up the hill, but just as the day was ending and he was reaching the top, the boulder rolled back down to the bottom. And then Sisyphus would have to start again the next day, and again, and again for the rest of his very long afterlife. Now that's a bad way to spend eternity.

Sisyphus's story is a popular one largely because it inspired a French philosopher named Albert Camus to write a famous essay about the nature of life. Camus thought that Sisyphus's punishment was symbolic of the struggles humans face every day. He called it "the absurdity of life." Camus thought that there are many days when things seem pointless, like pushing a rock up a hill when you know it's just going to roll back down. (Not quite sure how fun Camus was at parties.)

Camus may have made Sisyphus famous by turning him into a bummer of a metaphor, but we can't say his perspective on life is one we share. Consider thinking of life like a grand adventure (an odyssey, if you will) and not just a series of meaningless tasks. It's up to you to determine your own perspective.

**ALSO A WORD OF ADVICE: DON'T ANGER THE GODS. THEN LIFE REALLY WILL RESEMBLE PUSHING A LARGE ROCK UP A HILL!**

# CREATURES OF THE UNDERWORLD

The Underworld is known for being one of the scariest places in ancient Greece. But it's also one of the busiest. In addition to housing every mortal soul who ever lived, the Underworld is home to gods, goddesses, and many other spirits and beings. Governed by Hades and Persephone, the land of the dead features some of the creepiest creatures in Greek mythology.

## CHARON

If you were looking to get into the Underworld, you had to go through Charon first. As the official ferryman of the River Styx, Charon escorted newly dead souls over to Hades so the king of the dead could determine where they belonged in the Underworld. Many people left coins under the tongues of corpses as a way to pay Charon for his service and ensure their loved one was safely delivered to the land of the dead.

## CERBERUS

Cerberus was the official guard dog of the Underworld. With three gigantic heads and three mouths full of enormous teeth, he certainly did his job well. He's often referred to as the "hound of Hades," and we have it on record that he was the Underworld's goodest boy.

## THE FURIES

Also called the Erinyes or Eumenides, the Furies were deities of revenge and vengeance. They lived in the Underworld where they would punish evil souls for the terrible deeds they committed on Earth. While they were definitely scary creatures to come across, good and innocent people had nothing to fear from the Furies, as they were only interested in torturing souls who had committed terrible crimes.

## NYX AND EREBUS

Did you know that one of the happiest couples in Greek mythology took up residence in the Underworld? It's true! Nyx, the goddess of night, and Erebus, the god of darkness, chose to spend their happily ever after in the deepest and darkest part of the Underworld. Although the goddess of night wasn't evil, Nyx could still be quite intimidating.

# CHAPTER 15

# HALF-HORSING AROUND

This tale features an impressive cloud impersonation, really rude wedding guests, and lots of animal legs.

The centaur is one of the most famous and celebrated creatures in all of Greek mythology. The father of all of the centaurs was a sneaky but clever human king named Ixion, who was one of the few mortals who actually managed to talk their way onto Mount Olympus.

Ixion was not a very nice guy, to say the least. He murdered his own father-in-law and was shunned by both humans and gods. But he prayed and prayed and prayed to Zeus and somehow was granted forgiveness. (Probably because Zeus was flattered. You know he could never resist a good compliment.)

Zeus even invited Ixion up to Mount Olympus to dine with the Olympians! This was a *huge* honor and an amazingly lucky break for Ixion.

Not only had he avoided being punished by the gods, but he wound up getting invited over for dinner! You would think he'd be on his best behavior. But Ixion definitely forgot some basic rules of hanging out with gods. While he was on Olympus, Ixion fell madly in love with a beautiful goddess. Unfortunately, that goddess was married to Zeus. Ixion was crushing on Zeus's wife, Hera. Big mistake.

Ixion wasn't too great at hiding his feelings. Zeus discovered the scandal and decided to lay a trap for the lovestruck mortal. Zeus took a cloud and sculpted and molded it into the perfect likeness of Hera. Then he breathed life into the cloud and allowed it to walk around Olympus just like the real deal.

Ixion took the bait and immediately began to follow "Cloud Hera" all over Olympus. He fell for the trap hook, line, and sinker. He cornered the fake goddess and professed his love for her. He told Cloud Hera how he wanted to run away with her and get married. They could live together in a faraway kingdom and have a big, fluffy family. Of course, the cloud goddess said nothing in return, because, well, she was just a bunch of water droplets. But obviously, Ixion took her silence for a "yes" because he stole away with her and made a hasty escape from Olympus, running as far away as he could. He was foolish enough to think that he could hide from the king of the gods!

For a few months, Zeus toyed with Ixion and let the man think he had succeeded. Ixion married his cloud wife, and soon a baby was born. But Ixion was

ZEUS EVENTUALLY HUNTED DOWN IXION AND TRAPPED HIM IN THE UNDERWORLD. WE WON'T GET INTO DETAILS, BUT IT INVOLVES A WHEEL OF FIRE SPINNING FOR ALL ETERNITY, SO IT WASN'T A HAPPY ENDING FOR THAT GUY.

shocked when he saw that his newborn son was born as a half horse named Centaurus. Ixion was so offended by his existence that he banished his own son to live in the wild. While that was not a number one dad move, Centaurus actually grew strong and powerful, and during his life, he fathered many half-horse children all known as centaurs.

CENTAURS ARE HALF-HORSE, HALF-HUMAN CREATURES. THEY HAVE THE TORSO OF A PERSON, BUT THE BOTTOM HALF OF THEIR BODY RESEMBLES A HORSE.

Most of the centaurs lived in the mountains and forests of Thessaly in northern Greece. They shared this land with a kingdom of humans who were called the Lapiths, and they didn't always play nice with each other. For whatever reason, the Lapiths and the centaurs always seemed to have a beef with each other, and for years and years there was fighting.

Slowly but surely, things began to change. After a few years, an uneasy peace developed between the centaurs and the Lapiths. A lot of the peace and quiet was due to a young king named Pirithous. He spent his whole life watching the constant fighting between the centaurs and his people, and he wanted nothing more than to put an end to it. So when Pirithous ascended the throne, he worked to develop a good relationship with the king of the centaurs, and slowly the two tribes began to accept each other. Things were going along so well, in fact, that King Pirithous even invited the centaurs to his wedding to Princess Hippodamia! But unfortunately, this turned out to be a big mistake. Weddings usually involve drinks, dancing, and merriment, but sometimes guests can get a little unruly. And the centaurs were unruly to begin with. They probably didn't even make it through the first dance before everything went wrong. The centaurs started eating the wedding cake, dancing with the bridesmaids, throwing the bouquet—and eating the bouquet! It was tomfoolery that eventually turned into an all-out battle. Swords, shields, fists, and hooves pounded at each other, and when all was said and done, the Lapiths prevailed. The few remaining centaurs limped back into the woods and stayed away from Thessaly for a long time, leaving the Lapith Catering Company with a *lot* of cleaning up to do.

This event may have cemented the centaurs' bad reputation, but there were a few notable exceptions, specifically Chiron, the G.O.A.T. of all half-horse creatures.

Chiron wasn't just a centaur; he was a god. And he wasn't related to Ixion, which was a plus. His mother was a sea nymph named Philyra, and his father was Cronus, king of the Titans. This made Chiron immortal, just like his half brother Zeus and the other Olympians. Chiron's mother Philyra loved horses, so Cronus shape-shifted into one a lot to make her happy, and the baby was born part horse.

It was clear from the very beginning that Chiron was a bright young foal. As a student, he excelled in his studies in just about every subject: music,

medicine, hunting, and fighting. Chiron could do it all. And he loved learning. Some say his quest for knowledge was so great that he was tutored directly by Artemis and Apollo themselves!

Once he was old enough, Chiron took up residence on Mount Pelion and eventually became one of the greatest teachers of How to Be a Greek Hero 101. Heroes like Jason, Ajax, Asclepius, Achilles, and Heracles all learned from Chiron.

He had an amazing life and was an important part of some of the greatest heroic journeys in all of ancient Greece. Though he was supposed to be immortal, his life was cut short because of a tragic accident. And just like the wedding, it involved some unruly centaur party guests.

The great warrior Heracles was in from out of town visiting his old friend and teacher. Chiron was excited to see his student again and welcomed him with a lovely dinner party that included many four-legged guests, including another respected centaur named Pholus. They had a delightful meal and were just sitting down for drinks and dessert when a fight broke out among the centaurs.

Beautiful Jim Key was a famous horse who performed for audiences—even for U.S. presidents—in the early 1900s. He was supposedly trained to read and write, do math, and have political debates!

A great battle ensued, and poor Pholus was an early victim. The wild centaurs either didn't know or didn't care that they were challenging the great Heracles. They came at him relentlessly. Of course, Heracles was able to fight them off with ease and eventually used his bow and poisoned arrows to take them out one by one.

In a last-ditch effort, a wild centaur named Elatus charged at Heracles, swinging his club wildly. The hero turned quickly and ducked in time to avoid the blow. He quickly notched a poison arrow and shot Elatus through the arm, causing the centaur to drop his weapon. But Heracles was so strong that the arrow continued its flight, passing all the way through the centaur's arm and right into the knee of Chiron standing behind him!

The wise old centaur cried out in pain and dropped to the floor instantly. The poison from these arrows was so strong that Elatus died within seconds, but Chiron was not so lucky. Being an immortal, he wasn't able to die, so instead he wound up in constant and unbearable pain.

LIKE A LOT OF THESE MYTHS, THERE ARE A FEW DIFFERENT VERSIONS. SOME SAY THAT CHIRON'S PRAYERS TO ZEUS WERE NOT ENOUGH, SO HERACLES WENT TO HIS FATHER HIMSELF TO ARRANGE FOR CHIRON TO GIVE UP HIS IMMORTALITY. IN EXCHANGE FOR CHIRON'S SACRIFICE, HERACLES MADE A DEAL WITH ZEUS TO HAVE THE TITAN PROMETHEUS RELEASED FROM HIS ETERNAL TORTURE AND IMPRISONMENT.

For nine days, Heracles and bedridden Chiron tried to find a way to stop the poison and heal the wound. But it was impossible. Night after night, Chiron was wracked with pain. This was literally a fate worse than death. Chiron was in agony. In fact, it was so intense that he eventually prayed to Zeus, begging him to remove his immortality so that he could pass away and have the pain stop.

This wasn't a request Zeus was used to getting, but he could see the centaur's suffering. Reluctantly, Zeus removed the gift of immortality, and shortly thereafter, Chiron passed away, finally able to rest. But not wanting to lose him forever, the king of the gods placed Chiron's soul among the stars as the constellation known as Sagittarius.

To the Greeks, centaurs were important creatures that symbolized the inner battle humans sometimes fight against their more "animal" instincts. That's because, just like centaurs, we humans have a wild side! Sure, we don't have horse legs, but it's still tempting for us to act on impulse instead of thinking things all the way through. Acting on pure impulse can sometimes lead to mistakes and, well, ruining a wedding.

The Greeks celebrated intelligence and logical reasoning. In mythology some centaurs, like Chiron, exhibit these traits really well, showcasing the success of a creature guided by self-reflection. And some centaurs just act on instinct alone and cause a lot of trouble along the way. Be like Chiron and use logic before you act. (Oh, and don't get into fights at fancy weddings. It never ends well.)

CHIRON WAS A WISE FRIEND AND A GREAT TEACHER WHO PROBABLY EXCELLED AT GIVING HORSEBACK RIDES. BUT HIS MEMORY IS RESPECTED BECAUSE OF HIS ACTIONS IN LIFE, NOT HIS HORSE LEGS.

# CHAPTER 16

# THE PRINCESS, THE COW, AND THE GIANT WITH 100 EYES

This tale features badly behaved gods, transformation, a giant with lots of eyeballs, and a very long swim.

Everything was looking good for Io. She was a princess, she had lots of friends, and she even had a pretty cool job as a priestess to Hera. But Io's luck was about to run out. Like, big time.

Io had caught the eye of Zeus. And, of course, Zeus was already married to Hera, who was essentially Io's boss. Io tried her best to dodge the king of the gods, but he refused to give up. He took every opportunity he could to flirt with Io and try to romance her. At one point he even disguised himself as a cloud to hide and avoid being caught by Hera.

This was bad enough, but unfortunately, Io's problems were just getting started. One day, Zeus visited her in the temple of Hera. She tried to ignore him.

"Excuse me, I'm kind of busy here. I'm just, you know, dusting off the sculptures of your *wife* and everything."

Io continued her priestess duties—refilling incense, tidying up, dusting off the statues—and tried her best to ignore the king of the gods without appearing too disrespectful. But Zeus wasn't taking the hint. He continued to fawn all over Io and even started to tell her how much he loved her.

"You know, you've always been my favorite priestess," Zeus crooned. "Your beauty is next level."

But suddenly, out of nowhere, Hera materialized in the room!

Here's where it gets bad for Io. And kind of weird. Because without really thinking about it, Zeus cast a spell and transformed Io into a beautiful white cow. Yep, a *cow.*

"Zeus? What are you doing here?" Hera said, eying her husband suspiciously. Zeus had never visited her temple before.

"I was just, uh, looking at this cow!" replied the king of the gods.

"I heard you say 'favorite' and 'beauty.' Who were you talking to?"

"Oh, *definitely* this cow!" Zeus stammered. "I mean …
it's awesome, right? I mean look at those eyes! They're
so big! And cowy …"

But Hera didn't buy it. She knew something
was going on, and she had a pretty strong suspicion
about what it was. She just couldn't prove it.
Zeus would never appear in her temple without
a good reason.

"Yes, this certainly is a beautiful bovine," Hera
replied. "Very … cowy … indeed. I am so fortunate
to have worshipers who honor me with such a beautiful
gift. I will cherish it as a prized possession!"

IN ANCIENT GREECE, IT
WAS COMMON TO LEAVE
GIFTS FOR THE GODS
AT THEIR TEMPLES IN
EXCHANGE FOR BLESSINGS.
SOMETIMES, IT WAS FOOD
LIKE GRAINS, FRUITS,
HONEY, OR MILK; AND
SOMETIMES, THEY
ACTUALLY SACRIFICED
ANIMALS LIKE BIRDS AND
FISH. LEAVING A LIVE COW
IS PROBABLY A LITTLE
OVER THE TOP.

Well, now Zeus was in a real bind. He had turned
Io into a cow, and Hera thought it was a gift for her!
How was he ever going to get the princess back? For
her part, Hera decided that she was going to keep a
close eye on this cow. Or more accurately, eyes. And
lots of them.

Enter Argus Panoptes, the giant with a hundred
eyes. Argus was an old friend and servant to Hera. He
helped the Olympians fight against the Titans in a war
awhile back and had been loyally working for Hera ever
since. The queen of the gods figured he was perfectly
suited for the task of watching over this suspicious cow. She had a hunch
that her husband was going to try to steal it back, so Hera chained the
beautiful white cow to an olive tree near her temple and she instructed
Argus to watch over the cow.

"There's something fishy about this cow and I'm going to find out what it
is," Hera said. "Never take your eyes off it, Argus. All one hundred of them."

Hera ordered Argus to watch the animal at all times and to always be on
the lookout for someone who would want to steal this beautiful white cow.
Poor Io was stuck. She tried mooing, but, of course, no one could understand
her. After all, even gods don't speak cow.

Of course, Zeus had a pretty good idea of what Io the cow was trying to convey. But things were complicated. He wanted to rescue Io from her predicament, but he knew there was no way he could get near that cow with Argus constantly watching over it. So Zeus turned to his son and messenger, Hermes, for help. Hermes wasn't the biggest or the strongest of all the gods, but he was kind of a trickster. And this situation called for some clever thinking.

"Let me get this straight: You want me to help free your cow crush from a hundred-eyed giant?!" Hermes asked Zeus.

"Er, yes. That about sums it up."

"Eh, why not? Sounds like a fun way to spend an afternoon," Hermes said with a shrug. "One bovine intervention coming right up!"

Hermes disguised himself as a shepherd and pretended to accidentally stumble upon Argus and the white cow chained to the olive tree. "Wow, what a beautiful white cow!" Hermes exclaimed. "I *definitely* was not expecting to see that here!"

"It belongs to Hera, queen of the gods," the giant replied. "No touching."

"I wouldn't dream of it," Hermes replied. "I'm more of a sheep person, myself."

And with that, Hermes proceeded to set up camp just a few yards away from the olive tree. He kept his back to Argus to make it seem like he had no interest at all in the cow or the giant, but he knew he was being watched. Argus wasn't much of a talker, but he was *very* observant. Having a hundred eyes helps with that kind of stuff. But Hermes did his best to ignore the giant and went about the task of making a fire and setting up camp, all the while humming a quiet tune to himself.

Of course, Hermes had a plan. He wasn't just humming a regular song; he was actually casting a spell. His goal was to put Argus to

THE STAFF OF HERMES IS KNOWN AS A CADUCEUS. IT IS USUALLY DESCRIBED AS HAVING WINGS AND TWO SNAKES WRAPPED AROUND IT. THE CADUCEUS WAS GIVEN TO HERMES BY HIS BIG BROTHER APOLLO. IT WAS SORT OF A THANK-YOU PRESENT FOR HERMES BECAUSE HE HAD INVENTED THE MUSICAL INSTRUMENT WE CALL THE LYRE AND GIFTED IT TO APOLLO.

sleep so that he could untie the cow and return Io to Zeus. But this was easier said than done. Sometimes it's hard enough to get your own two eyes to close. Can you imagine what it's like to try to get a hundred eyes to shut? Especially when they are determined to stay awake and keep watch? The spell song simply wasn't cutting it.

So Hermes went for plan B. His magical staff had the power to put anyone to sleep just by touching them. The problem was that Argus wasn't just anyone. When Hermes snuck up to the giant to try to tap him with his staff, immediately Argus wheeled around and roared in outrage. So much for instant naptime.

The giant was drowsy and many of his eyes had already closed due to the song, but the few that remained open were focused on Hermes and full of fury. The messenger god swiftly moved out of reach of the giant and began hurling stones at him. The giant roared in anger and hurled stones back, but he was slow and weary from all the sleep magic. Eventually, Hermes had to fight the giant with his sword. It wasn't easy, but before long, Hermes slew Argus and unchained Io from the olive tree.

She was still a cow, but at least she was an unchained cow, and she had had it up to her horns with gods and giants. She swished her tail and bull-rushed away as fast as her hooves could carry her.

Hermes made his way back to Zeus, who was delighted. "You freed her! *Moo*-velous!"

But Zeus didn't have much time to enjoy the good news, because when Hera checked in on things

HERA WAS VERY GRATEFUL TO ARGUS FOR HIS DEDICATED SERVICE. SHE DECIDED TO PLACE HIS ONE HUNDRED EYES ON THE TAIL OF HER MOST SACRED BIRD, THE PEACOCK.

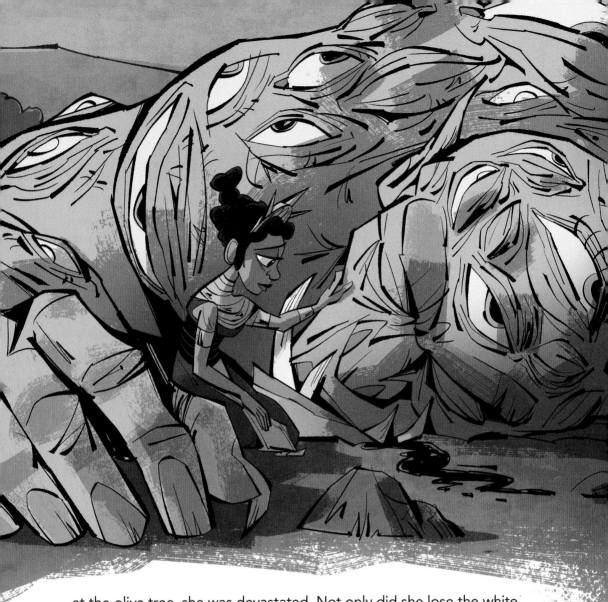

at the olive tree, she was devastated. Not only did she lose the white cow, but her faithful servant Argus was gone as well. Hera was furious, and she went straight to Zeus and demanded answers.

"What happened to my cow? And who killed my giant? And where on Earth is Io, the priestess?"

"I, uh—well, it's a long story. I might've accidentally turned Io into a cow and Hermes went to go get her and you know how these things go, my love."

"You turned her into a cow?!" Hera exclaimed. "That's a new low, even for you."

And even though Hera was livid at Zeus, she was also furious at Io. In her mind, the young priestess had betrayed her, and she wasn't going to let her go without at least some punishment. Plus, it was easier to get back at Io than it was to start a fight with Zeus.

So Hera enchanted a gadfly and instructed it to pursue and torment the cow priestess wherever she went. This might sound like kind of a small thing as far as divine punishments go, but if you've ever been annoyed by a fly buzzing around your head, you know how irritating these insects can be.

Eventually, Io swam out to the middle of the ocean to escape the annoying little bug. Legends say she did the bovine backstroke all the way to Egypt, where Zeus was able to pay her one last visit and transform her back into a human. There, Io lived out the rest of her life free from the annoyances of both gadflies and gods.

> The body of water that Io swam across is a bay of the Mediterranean Sea. It is still referred to today as the Ionian Sea in her honor.

Io really got the short end of the stick in this story. She should have never been turned into a cow in the first place—and not just because cows are a terrible disguise. Zeus should never have flirted with Io. She told him she wasn't interested, and he did not listen.

Respecting other people's boundaries and bodies is incredibly important. Unfortunately, consent is something that the Greek gods routinely ignored. This myth makes it clear that the gods were not always the good guys.

**I'VE ENCOUNTERED A LOT OF BUGS IN MY CIRCUITS, BUT NOTHING LIKE A GADFLY ...**

# CHAPTER 17

# CALYPSO'S LONELY ISLAND

> This tale features a possessive nymph-sorceress, a desperate king, a council of the gods, and a tale of unrequited love.

When the sorceress Calypso saw the giant storm coming, she was delighted. Storms brought shipwrecks, and shipwrecks often brought many strange and wonderful gifts to the shores of her remote island, Ogygia. Plus, the wind, rain, lightning, and thunder were all so exciting. Calypso lived alone, and anything that broke up the monotony of spending eternity on this island was welcome.

So when she saw a man floating in the water, the sorceress rushed down to the shore and pulled him onto the beach. He was thin but muscular, with a handsome face and a noble chin. Thankfully, he was still breathing, but just barely, so the sorceress used her magic to revive him. When he opened his eyes, she smiled down at him. He was so handsome!

"I am called Calypso," she said.

"Welcome to my island."

"I—I am Odysseus," the man said with a whisper.

"Welcome, Odysseus," Calypso said. "I think you will be very happy here. This island paradise will be your new home."

"My home … is … Ithaca," Odysseus replied weakly.

"Not anymore," Calypso said, smiling down at her handsome new friend.

The goddess Calypso was many things: immortal, a sorceress, a nymph, and the daughter of the Titan Atlas who held up the world. She was also really *bored*.

CALYPSO WAS IN SORT OF A COSMIC TIME OUT. BECAUSE SHE HAD SIDED WITH THE TITANS IN THEIR WAR WITH THE OLYMPIANS, ZEUS HAD SENTENCED CALYPSO TO AN ETERNITY OF LONELY ISLAND LIFE, WITH ONLY AN OCCASIONAL SHIPWRECKED SAILOR FOR COMPANY.

Forever is a very long time to be by yourself. But finally Calypso had a companion! And not just *any* companion. Odysseus was smart, funny, and handsome. It's no wonder Calypso fell for him immediately.

Calypso kept Odysseus as her companion for many years. She used magic to keep him happy and comfortable. But no matter how hard she tried, she could not convince him to choose to stay with her on his own.

"Calypso, it's been a blast, but I'd like to go home now," Odysseus said.

"Don't you want to stay here with me forever?" Calypso crooned. "It would be amazing! You, me, the whole island to ourselves?"

She even offered him immortality, but Odysseus turned it down. All he wanted to do was go home to his wife and family. This infuriated Calypso. She could use her magic to give him anything he wanted—why would he want to go home? She loved Odysseus, and she was not going to let him go. So he remained on the island for seven years.

Finally, after watching Odysseus stuck in Calypso's grasp, someone on Olympus decided it was time to intervene. The goddess Athena thought enough was enough and called a council of the gods to discuss bringing Odysseus home. She had a soft spot for the hero and was especially fond of his cleverness.

The gods assembled on Mount Olympus and listened to Athena as she made her plea. Odysseus was the *only* survivor of the Trojan War who had yet to return home, and she wanted to set that right. The council discussed

all of Odysseus's choices, good and bad. Athena didn't try to make it seem like Odysseus was perfect.

"Even *I* get angry at the king of Ithaca," she said. "He is far from perfect, but for each mistake he makes, he learns and tries to do better."

Many of the gods seemed to agree with that. As mortals go, Odysseus was quite popular among the Olympian gods. He was considered clever and wise and generally compassionate. But they weren't all sure if he should be let off the hook yet.

"Odysseus made a lot of mistakes," they countered. "Look what he did to poor Poseidon's son!"

Athena used that to her advantage. "Well then, it's obvious how we must proceed," the goddess of wisdom explained. "From this day forward, we shall allow no mortal king to be kind, wise, or just in the way Odysseus has been. And if anyone makes a mistake, he must be punished forever. Even if he pays for his mistakes and overcomes them with cleverness, determination, and honor, as

ODYSSEUS HAD BLINDED POLYPHEMUS, AN ANGRY ONE-EYED CYCLOPS, WHILE ESCAPING FROM HIS CAVE. UNFORTUNATELY FOR ODYSSEUS, POLY-PHEMUS JUST HAPPENED TO BE POSEIDON'S SON. SEE PAGE 87 FOR A REFRESHER.

Odysseus has done, that will not be taken into account."

The other gods began to look awkwardly around the room. That wasn't what they were saying, was it?

"In fact," Athena continued, "any ruler who displays this kind of intelligent or compassionate behavior should be condemned by the gods immediately!"

Suddenly, there was a whole lot of hemming and hawing in the council hall on Olympus. Some of the gods objected, and others began to backtrack a little, softening their stance on Odysseus.

"I mean, it's not like he's *that* bad."

"Yeah, Poseidon oughta give the guy a break!"

But Zeus spoke up and quieted the group. "You have made your point, Athena, and made it well," he said. "It is time to bring Odysseus home."

Zeus summoned Hermes, messenger of the gods, and instructed him to fly to Ogygia. "Tell Calypso that Zeus instructs her to release Odysseus."

When Hermes reached the island of Ogygia, he found the great Odysseus, king of Ithaca and hero of Greece, curled up in a ball on the beach, weeping into the sand. This was definitely a low point for the clever king.

"I just want to go home!" Odysseus bawled.

The exact location of Ogygia is uncertain, but some sources suggest it may have been the current island of Othonoi, which is the westernmost point in modern-day Greece. The only way to reach it is by boat.

"All right, buddy, time to dry those tears," Hermes said and then cleared his throat. "Stand and be comforted, for I come with great news. Zeus has decreed that—after seven years—Calypso must finally release you from this enchanted island and allow you to return home."

Odysseus stood, wiping the sand from his face and blinking as he stared at the Olympian before him. "Wait," he stammered. "You mean I've been on this island for *seven years*?!" And again, he began to wail. "I knew it was a long time, but … seven years?!"

Hermes decided it was best to let Odysseus work through this one on his own. "Uh, I'm just gonna go have a chat with Calypso," the messenger said. "I'll be right back. Don't go anywhere."

"Where am I gonna go?!" roared Odysseus.

"Er, right. Well, you know what I mean."

And with that, Hermes zipped away from the beach to confront Calypso and deliver the news from Zeus.

"Hermes," Calypso said in her rich, beautiful voice. She didn't show even a trace of surprise that the messenger of the gods was in her home. "I assume you have come here with news from Olympus."

"I have, Calypso," he replied and explained that she must release Odysseus.

Calypso sighed a heavy sigh and looked up from her loom. She was distractingly beautiful, as many nymphs were. Sparkling eyes, flowing hair, and a voice like warm honey. "As I thought. As much as I wish him to marry me, the man refuses. He is as stubborn as he is loyal. But still, he is mine, and I do not wish to give him up."

Hermes told Calypso that she did not have much choice in the matter. This was a decree from Zeus himself, and he would not be refused.

"Oh, Zeus? Why didn't you *say* so?" The nymph laughed sarcastically. "Of course we will do whatever Zeus says. Zeus is the king of the gods! Zeus gets to do whatever he wants whenever he wants! Women like me don't get the same opportunities, do we?"

"That's not really for me to say." Hermes was getting a little uncomfortable. Calypso clearly had a point there. This was not how he imagined this conversation going.

"Do you love Odysseus?" the messenger asked.

"Of course I love him," Calypso replied. "Can't you see everything I do for him?"

"But do you *truly* love him?" Hermes asked again.

Calypso let those words sink in and then replied simply. "Yes."

"Then how can you keep him here against his will?"

"Very well," said Calypso. "I will release him. But only because I choose to. I am nothing if not compassionate. So be it."

Hermes left the cave and returned to the beach to find that Odysseus had collected himself and seemed a bit more composed. "I have spoken to Calypso," Hermes said. "At the instruction of Zeus, she has agreed to release you as her prisoner. She will allow you to sail home and be reunited once again with your family."

Odysseus could hardly believe what he was hearing. After all he had been through, it took him some time to process what Hermes was telling him. "I am really going home?" he said slowly.

"You are," the god replied.

Calypso stood on the beach and hugged Odysseus one last time as he prepared to build a raft and make his journey home. After her talk with Hermes, she decided that she could not, in good conscience, keep him prisoner any longer. The fact that Zeus had demanded his release had nothing to do with her change of heart. After all, it was only her magic that kept Odysseus happy during his time in captivity. She realized that no matter how much she tried to charm him into staying, he never really wanted to be with her in the first place.

"Alas, Odysseus," the nymph said tearfully, "I am afraid our love was just not meant to be. It is time for you to return home to your

THERE ARE DIFFERENT VERSIONS OF CALYPSO'S BACKSTORY. BUT ACCORDING TO HOMER, CALYPSO WAS A NYMPH AND ALSO A DEMI-TITAN, WHICH HELPS EXPLAIN HER MAGICAL POWERS. OTHER WRITERS SAY SHE WAS A SEA NYMPH OR ONE OF THE NEREIDS—BUT WE WILL STICK WITH HOMER BECAUSE I LIKE DOING THINGS BY THE BOOK. (SEE WHAT I DID THERE?)

family. I know it will be hard for you, but try to move on and live your life."

Odysseus took a deep breath and bowed graciously. "Thank you, Calypso. And thank you, Lord Hermes. I cannot believe that I am finally going home!"

With that, the king of Ithaca set sail for the shores of his homeland. Okay, "sailing" might be a strong word. He had no ship, no crew, and practically no supplies, but as Odysseus pushed his leaky raft out beyond the waves, he felt like he was on a luxury cruise. He was going home! And that was all that mattered.

You might think that's the end of Odysseus's story, but it is not. Even after he made it home to the island of Ithaca, his struggles continued. He had to claim his kingdom back from a number of suitors who were all trying to marry his wife and take the throne. Homer is the OG of the it-ain't-over-till-it's-over technique and really puts Odysseus through the ringer. This story reminds us to never give up hope. You never know when Hermes is on his way to rescue you!

IT TOOK ODYSSEUS 10 YEARS TO TRAVEL THE SAME DISTANCE THAT THE OTHER GREEKS COVERED IN SIX MONTHS. I ONCE WAITED AN HOUR FOR A VIDEO TO DOWNLOAD. I KNOW IT'S NOT THE SAME THING, BUT I DID NOT GIVE UP HOPE!

# WISH YOU WERE HERE! ODYSSEUS'S EPIC ROAD TRIP

After the Trojan War was over, Odysseus and his crew headed home on one of the longest journeys in all of Greek mythology. Here's a timeline of all the places Odysseus stopped on his way home to Ithaca, as well as some of the obstacles he faced along the way.

**1. LAND OF THE CICONES:** First, the crew made a quick pit stop for food and water. Unfortunately, they raided the town and took all its gold and supplies. This angered the gods.

**2. ISLAND OF THE LOTUS-EATERS:** Odysseus and his crew managed to leave the island of the Lotus-Eaters by shaking off the flowers' hypnotizing spell, but it was a close call. (See page 35.)

**3. ISLAND OF THE CYCLOPES:** The crew was captured by the cyclops Polyphemus, but Odysseus's cleverness helped them to escape. If only he hadn't given the giant his real name! (See page 87.)

**4. FLOATING CITY OF AEOLIA:** Odysseus and his crew arrived at a floating city where the king gave him a magic bag of wind to help them sail straight to Ithaca. But when the crew accidentally let out too much wind, they were redirected straight back to the floating city. This was when Odysseus started to realize that he might have angered the gods just a tad.

**5. LAND OF THE LAESTRYGONIANS:** Nothing says epic journey like escaping a ferocious tribe of human-eating giants! Odysseus and a few men managed to escape, but much of his crew perished.

GERMANY
SWITZERLAND
FRANCE
ITALY
SPAIN
The Underworld
Island of the Phaeacians
12
7
Tyrrhenian Sea
6
Aeaea
8
11
Siren Songs
Ogygia
5
Aeolia
Land of the Laestrygonians
ALGERIA
TUNISIA
2
Island of the Lotus-Eaters

NORTH AMERICA
ARCTIC OCEAN
ASIA
ATLANTIC OCEAN
EUROPE
Area enlarged above
INDIAN OCEAN
AFRICA

**6. ISLAND OF AEAEA:** Odysseus and his crew stopped for supplies on the island of Aeaea and met the sorceress Circe. Despite the fact that she temporarily turned his men into pigs, Odysseus and Circe fell in love. But after a year, Odysseus decided to return to Ithaca anyway.

**7. THE UNDERWORLD:** Circe advised Odysseus to sail with his crew to the edge of the Underworld to speak with the ghost of a prophet named Tiresias. They did, and got invaluable advice on how to get home.

**8. SIREN SONGS:** Thanks to Tiresias, Odysseus knew how to avoid the Sirens' hypnotizing songs and was able to sail straight past the dangerous group of man-eating monsters.

**9. SCYLLA AND CHARYBDIS:** A sea monster on one side and a deadly whirlpool on the other! This trap almost took out Odysseus and his crew, but they managed to pull off a narrow escape—although they did lose six men in the process.

**10. ISLAND OF HELIOS:** On Helios's island, the crew killed one of his precious cows. Do *not* mess with gods and their cows! A storm drowned the remaining crew members, and only Odysseus survived.

**11. ISLAND OF OGYGIA:** Odysseus wound up on the island of Ogygia, home to the sorceress Calypso. He was held here for seven years until Zeus ordered Calypso to set the hero free. (See page 143.)

**12. ISLAND OF THE PHAEACIANS:** Finally back on track, Odysseus stopped at the Island of the Phaeacians. He told them his whole story, and they were so moved that they provided him with a speedy ship and escorted him back to Ithaca.

**13. ITHACA:** Cue the confetti! Odysseus finally, finally made it home.

# MISSION: RESCUE ZEUS

This tale features a giant monster with snakes for limbs, a thunderbolt shortage, the separation of a god from his muscles, and a mythological grandpa rescue.

n Mount Olympus, there's pretty much only one god who gets to do whatever he wants: Zeus. As the king of the gods and head honcho, very few people or creatures were willing to challenge him. And almost no one was able to defeat him in battle. That was until Zeus met his match.

Enter Typhon, one of the scariest monsters in ancient Greece. He had enormous wings and was so tall that his heads touched the sky and stars. He had the torso of a man, but his legs and arms were made up of coiled vipers that would hiss and attack as he moved.

And in case snake-limbs weren't intimidating enough, he also had multiple dragon-heads with glowing red eyes that could paralyze his opponents with fear. Oh, and he could breathe fire. Basically, Typhon was so scary that he was sometimes called "the father of all monsters." Yikes.

Typhon was pretty fierce, and he knew it. Because he was so scary and powerful, naturally he had a burning desire to take control of the cosmos. This was bad news for the Olympians. Many of them were (rightfully) terrified of Typhon. But not Zeus. The king of the gods was way too proud to act even a little intimidated by some overblown monster with a snake obsession.

Over the years, Zeus and Typhon had some pretty legendary battles. Typhon was determined to win the crown, but Zeus refused to give in. They went toe-to-toe several times, and during their final fight, Typhon was actually able to get the better of Zeus.

Determined to steal the throne from Zeus, Typhon had launched an all-out attack on the king of the gods. The two had been trading blows for almost a full day. Typhon lashed out at Zeus with his snake limbs and spit fire at the god over and over. Zeus responded with thunderbolt after thunderbolt. The relentless rain of lightning easily repelled the snaky giant.

Things were looking good for Zeus—until he ran out of thunderbolts. He searched frantically in his quiver for one more, but it was no use. He was fresh out. And without a way to defend himself, suddenly Zeus was in big trouble. Typhon quickly scaled the mountain Zeus had perched himself on and overpowered the Olympian.

Typhon knew he couldn't kill Zeus (being immortal kind of takes that off the table), so he decided to work up a special kind of punishment for him. Typhon dragged Zeus to a cave on the side of a mountain … where he proceeded to take the god's body apart. *Yuck.*

Red spitting cobras can very accurately spray venom and hit their target from up to eight feet (2.4 m) away. These snakes aim for the eyes of their predators or prey to blind them.

PART OF THE REASON TYPHON WAS ANGRY WITH ZEUS WAS BECAUSE OF THE TITAN VERSUS OLYMPIAN WAR. ZEUS AND THE OLYMPIANS STOLE THE THRONE FROM THE TITANS AND LOCKED MANY OF THEM UP IN TARTARUS, THE PRISON OF THE UNDERWORLD. MANY OF THOSE TITANS WERE TYPHON'S HALF-SIBLINGS, AND HE WANTED TO GET REVENGE ON THEIR BEHALF.

Typhon left Zeus's skin and bones intact, but pulled off his muscles and tendons so the god could not escape. Zeus, quite literally, couldn't move a muscle.

Typhon kept Zeus there for weeks so he could tease and torture him whenever he felt like it. And poor Zeus was not holding up well. His cries of pain and outrage echoed down from the mountain and across the countryside, where they were heard by Pan, a god and satyr (see page 95 for more of Pan's story). Being a musical fellow (he was always carrying his pan flute), this terrible bellowing was impossible for Pan to ignore. He immediately sought out his father, Hermes, to see if he knew what all the ruckus was about.

PAN'S FATHER IS HERMES, AND HERMES' FATHER IS ZEUS, WHICH MAKES ZEUS PAN'S GRANDFATHER. HOWEVER, IT IS NOT KNOWN WHETHER ZEUS PREFERRED "GRANDPA," "POP-POP," OR "GRANDDAD."

Hermes was aware of Zeus's situation. Like many of the other Olympians, he felt terrible for the king of the gods, but he was also terrified of Typhon. If he got involved, he could wind up just like Zeus! But Pan wouldn't let it go.

"Isn't there anything we can do to help? We aren't just gonna leave Grandpa Zeus up there like that, are we?"

The satyr asked question after question until eventually Hermes realized he would have to do something. He couldn't let his fear stop him from trying to save Zeus.

"All right, fine," he replied. "I'll think of something."

The father-son duo concocted a plan. Once darkness fell, Hermes used his winged sandals to fly Pan up the side of the cliff. Then, the pair snuck into the dark cave. They could hear the loud, heavy breathing of Typhon as he slept, sprawled across the top of the mountain above them. In the dim light, Hermes and Pan could just barely make out the limp form of Zeus chained to the far wall.

The father and son tiptoed across the cave to Zeus and silently began working on putting their king's body back together. Hermes found the tendons in a small sack on the floor, and Pan found the muscles in a large chest. Together, the pair worked through the night to rebuild Zeus, hoping all the while that the beast above them would not wake up. After a few hours, all of Zeus's muscles and tendons were back in place and he was able to stand and walk a bit. In a flash, Hermes grabbed his father around the shoulders and returned the god back to Olympus, where he was able to heal properly.

A tendon is a connective tissue that attaches muscle to bone or other structures in the human body.

Now, as you might imagine, Typhon was more than a little bit upset. He roared with rage when he discovered that his prisoner had somehow escaped, but he knew without a doubt where Zeus had gone. Typhon decided it was time to bring the fight to Zeus, and so he slowly and methodically began climbing Mount Olympus.

True to form, most of the other Olympian gods were so scared that they began to flee. This time, they each took animal forms and flew all the way to Egypt. And Zeus was tempted to join them. In fact, he got ready to change into his majestic animal form—an eagle—by stretching his arms and practicing his fearsome eagle cry!

But then he saw that Athena, goddess of war and wisdom, was staying behind in her human form to face the monster. In her enchanted armor, she hurled spears and rocks at Typhon as he climbed the mountain toward the gods' palace. She also didn't miss the opportunity to mock the other gods for fleeing like cowards.

Maybe this was what kept Zeus from leaving. If anyone had a reason to fear Typhon, it would be him, right? But seeing his daughter standing alone on the cliff battling the giant monster was too much for Zeus. He transformed into a mighty eagle, but instead of flying away, he made a brief pit stop in Hephaestus's workshop to load up on thunderbolts and then flew to the top of a nearby mountain. After getting himself settled, he quickly changed back into big, bad Zeus and began hurling thunderbolts at Typhon while Athena held the monster back.

It was actually a pretty good strategy! With Athena holding her ground, Typhon was an easy target. And when the monster realized that Zeus was not only fully healed but also stocked up on weapons, he was terrified! Eventually, Typhon fell to the ground, defeated. Quickly, Zeus and Athena hurled the monster's body into the deep, bottomless pit of Tartarus. Then, for good measure, Zeus moved an entire mountain, Mount Etna, over the opening to keep Typhon imprisoned forever.

And that's why you don't mess with the king of the gods.

MOUNT ETNA IS AN ACTUAL ACTIVE VOLCANO ON THE ITALIAN ISLAND OF SICILY. THIS IS NOT THE ONLY STORY WHERE A GIANT BEAST GETS IMPRISONED BENEATH IT. IT'S PROBABLY PRETTY CROWDED UNDER THERE—NO WONDER ETNA ERUPTS FROM TIME TO TIME.

This is a popular story in Greek mythology because it shows how even the biggest, baddest gods on Mount Olympus could still lose a battle from time to time.

No matter how brave, strong, or famous you are, you will still encounter challenges in your life. Sometimes you will have a bad day. Sometimes things will go wrong. Sometimes a large snake-like monster will lock up your muscles in a chest. (Okay, hopefully not that last one.)

When this happens, remember that everyone struggles. Loss is a part of life. We will all know the taste of defeat at some point. No one is untouchable, not even Zeus!

ASKING FOR HELP IS NOT ALWAYS EASY, BUT IT IS IMPORTANT. EVERYONE NEEDS A LITTLE ASSIST NOW AND THEN. WHERE WOULD I BE WITHOUT MY EXTENSION CORD?

# CHAPTER 19

# MOTHER OF A WARRIOR

This tale features gods threatened by greatness, a shape-shifting nymph, a mother's love, and the world's most iconic heel.

Thetis was a sea nymph, or a goddess of the water. She was known for many things: her passion, her intelligence, and her loyalty to those she loved. But most of all, she was known for her mesmerizing beauty. She was, without a doubt, one of the most stunning sea nymphs to ever swim in the ocean.

Thetis even caught the eye of two of Greece's most powerful gods, Zeus and Poseidon. Both were strong-willed and a little arrogant, and neither one of them had much experience with not getting what they wanted. So the brothers weren't exactly thrilled when they realized that they would have to compete against each other for Thetis's affection.

"Poseidon?! What are you doing here? Why are you trying to talk to Thetis? You know I'm into her!"

"But I saw her first!"

This competition went on for a long time. Neither one of the gods was willing to back down. But while the two brothers were arguing over Thetis, a prophecy was revealed. It said that Thetis would one day have a son who would grow up to become a great warrior.

Now, in theory, that all sounds great. Who wouldn't want their son to become an impressive warrior? But here's where it gets tricky. The prophecy then went on to say that Thetis's son would become even greater than his father and would be forever known for his glory. For gods like Zeus and Poseidon, having a son who would grow up to surpass them was pretty much a worst-case scenario. They were not interested in being over-shadowed by their own offspring.

THETIS HELPED RESCUE ANOTHER FAMOUS OLYMPIAN, HEPHAESTUS. WHEN HERA KICKED HEPHAESTUS OUT OF MOUNT OLYMPUS AFTER HIS BIRTH, THETIS RESCUED THE BABY FROM THE SEA AND HELPED HIM FIND A HOME ON LAND.

"On second thought, you can have her after all," Zeus said to his brother.

"Ah come on, Zeus! You really think anyone could be more powerful than *you*? What are you, chicken?"

The more the two brothers thought about it, the more it became clear that any godly union with Thetis would be downright reckless. If Thetis married a god, her son would grow up to be immortal. And a powerful immortal god could be dangerous for everybody, especially for those at the top of the system like Zeus and Poseidon. What if they were overthrown by this powerful warrior?

"It's simple, really," Zeus explained to Poseidon. "Thetis cannot marry a god. It could cause too much trouble. She has to marry a mortal instead. Her son may grow up to be a mighty warrior, but at least we know that his reign and power will be limited."

Zeus and Poseidon encouraged mortals across the land to marry Thetis. It shouldn't have been a hard sell: Thetis was a beautiful sea nymph, after all. The thing was, Thetis also had a reputation for being stubborn and short-tempered. To complicate things even more, Thetis did not have any interest in getting married, especially to a mere mortal.

And just in case that didn't make arranging a marriage hard enough, Thetis was also a shape-shifter. She'd been known to transform into terrifying beasts just to scare suitors away. This could make it hard for a guy to have a conversation with her.

SOME MORTALS ARE CONCERNED WITH THE IDEA OF LEAVING BEHIND A LEGACY. THIS CONCEPT DOESN'T APPLY TO GODS BECAUSE THEY ARE IMMORTAL AND WILL LIVE FOREVER. THERE IS NO NEED TO MAKE SURE THEY ARE REMEMBERED. LEAVING BEHIND A LEGACY IS A DISTINCTLY HUMAN DESIRE, AND IT WAS A VERY IMPORTANT CONCEPT BACK IN ANCIENT GREECE.

Yet there was one man who wasn't discouraged by Thetis and her transformation skills: Peleus, the king of Phthia. Unlike Zeus and Poseidon, Peleus wasn't at all concerned about the prospect of his future son transcending him in strength and power. In fact, he was pretty stoked about the idea of having a famous, powerful kid. If his son would always be remembered, then so would he.

But Peleus still had to get Thetis to agree to marry him. And it wasn't going to be easy. He tried to approach Thetis and have a conversation, but she always ran away or shape-shifted before he got the chance. After a few months, Peleus was starting to get fed up. He had to find a way to talk to the sea nymph.

The world's largest single cave passage, located in Vietnam, could fit an entire New York City block inside it, complete with 40-story skyscrapers.

One night, he waited in a cave by the sea that Thetis was known to sleep in. When she finally drifted off, Peleus took the opportunity to block the mouth of the cave with a giant boulder and trap her inside with him. When she woke up, Thetis was furious.

"How dare you capture me? You are just a mortal! Let me out immediately!"

"I'd be happy to. Just agree to marry me and we'll be on our way," he replied.

Thetis tried to shape-shift and escape.

First, she turned into a bird so she could fly far away from Peleus, but there was no way out of the cave. Then, she became a roaring lion, but Peleus didn't budge.

Thetis continued to turn into animal after animal, but she couldn't find a way out of the cave. Peleus refused to back down, even when Thetis transformed into animals with rather sharp teeth. She even tried turning into fire, but Peleus still refused to yield. Unless Thetis was willing to actually kill Peleus, there was no way out of the cave. And so, with no way out, Thetis decided to consider Peleus's marriage proposal.

*The prophecy foretold that I'm going to have a son, so I am going to have to marry someone eventually,* she thought to herself. *At least this one is clever. Maybe marrying him wouldn't be so terrible. Especially if he's willing to negotiate.*

THE WEDDING OF THETIS AND PELEUS IS ONE OF THE MOST FAMOUS WEDDINGS IN GREEK MYTHOLOGY. AND BECAUSE OF A HEATED ARGUMENT OVER WHO WAS THE MOST BEAUTIFUL GODDESS, IT'S KNOWN FOR BEING THE CATALYST OF THE TROJAN WAR. WHAT CAN WE SAY? CRAZY THINGS ALWAYS HAPPEN AT WEDDINGS.

Thetis decided she would marry Peleus, but only if he would agree to some conditions. "I will marry you only if you consider our marriage to be more of a business arrangement," Thetis stated. "I do not love you and never will. And I want to be able to come to the sea whenever I please."

Peleus agreed. "Sounds reasonable to me!"

"And one more thing: I want to have a child."

Peleus wanted that as well, and the two were married within the week.

And for a while, they had a relatively pleasant marriage—er, business arrangement. Thetis got to enjoy the sea, and Peleus was pleased knowing that he was married to a beautiful sea nymph that so many men pined after. Before long, they had a child together: a boy named Achilles.

Achilles was a delightful baby. His parents adored him, especially Thetis. Her maternal love for him was fierce and all-consuming. She adored everything about him. There was just one problem: He wasn't immortal.

Of course, Thetis had known this was going to be the case, considering he had a mortal father. But she wasn't prepared for just how protective she would feel over her child. She felt physically ill when she thought of anything bad happening to him. She decided she would do whatever it took to make him immortal. It was her duty as a mother.

So one night, Thetis carried a sleeping Achilles and made the dangerous journey to the River Styx, one of the rivers of the Underworld. In addition to being incredibly creepy and filled with dead souls, it also happened to have the power to grant immortality—which is exactly what Thetis was after.

Of course, being a baby, Achilles couldn't swim, so Thetis had to hold him by the foot and dip him into the river. She managed to get his entire body submerged except for the one teeny tiny part she was holding: his heel.

Because of his dunk in the River Styx, Achilles was more or less invulnerable, and Thetis felt confident that her plan to protect her son had worked. Yes, he had that one little weak spot. But he was perfectly safe as long as his heel wasn't injured. It seemed like pretty good odds to Thetis. After all, how often do you injure your heel?

For a while, Thetis, Peleus, and Achilles tried to make things work as a traditional family. But as time went on, it became clear that Thetis wasn't cut out for land life (and she wasn't that big a fan of her husband, either). She yearned to go back to the sea, and eventually, she decided to live there permanently.

The Achilles tendon connects your heel bone to your calf muscles. It is the strongest tendon in the human body, enabling a person to stand on their toes and push off the ground to walk.

But Thetis never stopped watching over or protecting Achilles. She kept a close eye on her son and did whatever was necessary to keep him safe. This proved to be a difficult job, as Achilles grew to become one of the greatest warriors in ancient Greece.

Thetis anxiously watched Achilles as he fought in the Trojan War. People were amazed

by his skill and strength as a warrior, but Thetis was never able to fully relax. She knew that Achilles had a weak spot, and she was worried that it was just a matter of time before someone found it.

THIS IS WHERE THE PHRASE "ACHILLES' HEEL" COMES FROM. IT REFERS TO A PERSON'S PARTICULAR WEAK SPOT.

And sadly, she was right. Despite being the best soldier on either side, Achilles was killed in the Trojan War. He was shot by Paris, the prince of Troy. Many people would consider it a bad shot, but for Achilles, it was deadly. The arrow hit him right in the heel.

Most people remember Achilles as one of the greatest warriors in ancient Greece. He had a reputation for being impressive, intimidating, and fierce. After all, Achilles was the best on the battlefield in the Trojan War.

But not many people realize that Achilles was so dominating because his mother had risked everything to keep him safe. If Thetis hadn't dunked Achilles in the River Styx, who knows how long he would've survived?

It's important to remember that a hero is more than who they are on the battlefield. Every hero has loved ones who care about them. After all, even warriors need help from their mom sometimes.

I DO NOT HAVE HEELS (OR ANY BODY PARTS AT ALL), BUT SOMETIMES I REGRET NOT HAVING FEET. THEN I REMEMBER THAT EACH FOOT HAS AROUND 7,000 NERVE ENDINGS, MAKING THEM EXTREMELY SENSITIVE TO TOUCH AND PAIN, AND I DECIDE I AM FINE AS I AM.

# CHAPTER 20

# A RIDDLE WRAPPED IN A SNAKE'S TAIL

This tale features an overly intelligent monster with animal body parts, a city desperately in need of a hero, ridiculously difficult riddles, and a very sore loser.

The kingdom of Thebes was under attack. Which was a pity, really, because it used to be a glorious place. It had marble statues, a bustling marketplace, and a beautiful countryside. But the kingdom had a bit of a problem—a monster problem.

Now, any monster would be bad enough, but this one was particularly troublesome. The Sphinx was a giant monster with the body of a lion, the head of a woman, the wings of an eagle, and a snake for a tail. She was a little bit extra.

And while her physical appearance was intimidating to say the least, the Sphinx was known for something even more dangerous: her intelligence.

Her favorite activity was tormenting travelers who were passing through the city of Thebes. These people would be minding their own business, when suddenly they'd hear the sound of wings.

Before they could process what was happening, they found themselves face-to-face with the ferocious Sphinx.

"Hello there," she'd say in her singsong voice.

Now most of these unlucky travelers would be trembling in their boots—a winged monster with the head of a woman and the body of a lion will do that to you. Not to mention the snake tail. But some managed to find a way to gather their courage and greet the Sphinx.

> THE SPHINX WAS THE DAUGHTER OF TWO OTHER FAMOUS MONSTERS: ORTHUS, A GIANT DOG WITH TWO HEADS, AND ECHIDNA, A HALF WOMAN, HALF SNAKE. SHE'S ALSO THE SIBLING TO THE GORGONS AND THE FAMOUS CHIMERA MONSTER. YOU DON'T WANT TO VISIT THIS FAMILY OVER THE HOLIDAYS.

"Hello, Ms. Lion-Winged-Monster-With-A-Snake-Tail-Lady-Monster-Thing. May I please pass?"

"Of course," the Sphinx would purr. "You are welcome to pass as soon as you play a little game with me."

"I'm afraid I'm not a fan of games, ma'am."

"A riddle, then. Please, I insist."

And because most of the travelers didn't have the skills or ability to fight back against such a complicated monster, they decided to take a stab at solving the Sphinx's riddle. After all, it was just a riddle. How hard could it be?

Very hard, as it turns out.

"Which creature has only one voice, but has four feet in the morning, two feet in the afternoon, and three feet at night?" the Sphinx asked and smiled.

None of the travelers the Sphinx encountered knew the answer. But some of the braver ones managed to squeak out a reply.

"I don't know, ma'am. Maybe one of your monster friends?"

"Pity," the Sphinx replied. "I rather liked your manners."

And with that, the Sphinx would attack the traveler and swallow them whole.

Now the king of Thebes, a mortal named Creon, was not a fan of this new tourist attraction.

"Visitors of Thebes are being *eaten* by a monster! This isn't good for business!"

Creon had a point, and Thebes quickly became known as a place you *don't* want to go. This wasn't a good look for King Creon.

The king tried everything he could think of to get rid of the Sphinx. He sent his best soldiers to fight her. He sent his wisest men to solve her riddles. He even prayed to the gods. But none of those things helped. The Sphinx devoured the soldiers and the scholars alike. Even the gods turned their back on Thebes.

"Sorry, dude, you're on your own," Zeus replied. "I've got my own monsters to deal with."

King Creon was at the end of his rope. No one was willing to help him defeat the Sphinx.

Desperate, he decided to play his final bargaining chip.

"Anyone who can rid us of the Sphinx can have my throne and become the new king," he declared.

But even that didn't work on the people of Thebes. They knew that they would never get out alive.

But there was one man who thought he might be up for the challenge. His name was Oedipus.

Before arriving in Thebes, Oedipus had been totally unaware of the whole Sphinx situation. He had simply been passing through the city of Thebes. Luckily, he

SOME VERSIONS OF THIS MYTH CLAIM THAT THE GODDESS HERA SENT THE SPHINX TO THEBES AS PUNISHMENT FOR AN ANCIENT CRIME. HERA REALLY NEEDS TO WORK ON HER ANGER MANAGEMENT SKILLS.

managed to avoid the Sphinx and walked right into the heart of the city, no problem.

"You, sir, are one lucky guy," the local innkeeper told him. "We've been having a little bit of a monster problem lately."

"Monster problem?" Oedipus replied.

"Yeah, you know. The Sphinx? Lion monster with a snake tail and a genius complex?"

"Never heard of her."

"Well, she has been attacking tourists left and right. And no one has been able to solve her riddles. The king is so upset that he's offering his throne to the person who can defeat her."

Now this was appealing to Oedipus. He was in the market for a new place to live. And being king didn't sound too shabby. Plus, he considered himself to be a smart sort of fellow—certainly smart enough to outwit a monster. Maybe he would give it a shot.

"This Sphinx … she's often found on the outskirts of the city, you say?"

"Oh, yes. You're lucky to have made it in alive. She was probably terrorizing someone else that day."

The next morning, Oedipus got up bright and early to do a little monster fighting. He had no idea what to expect. Up until now, he had thought of riddles as fun childhood brainteasers—certainly not something to be scared of. But maybe he was underestimating the whole situation. If the king was willing to give up the throne to defeat her, this must be a pretty bad monster.

Oedipus took a deep breath and gathered up his courage. He was ready.

Oedipus began walking toward the city limits, and once he was at the outskirts of Thebes, he cried out to the monster.

"Oh, Sphinxy, I heard a rumor that you are giving out riddles. I'd like to try one!"

There is also a famous sphinx in Egypt. The Great Sphinx of Giza is a gigantic limestone statue with the body of a lion and the head of a human. Unlike the Greek Sphinx, the ancient Egyptian sphinxes were considered spiritual guardians.

And of course, when the Sphinx heard the arrogance in Oedipus's voice, she had no choice but to fly right over.

*I'll give him something to laugh about,* she thought.

Out of nowhere, the Sphinx leaped upon him, pinning him to the ground with her gigantic lion paws.

Oedipus couldn't help it; he let out a terrified scream as the Sphinx's snake tail hissed and bared its fangs.

"Um, yes, hello there, ma'am," he sputtered. "I was hoping we could chat in a more … civilized fashion."

Reluctantly, the Sphinx removed her paws, freeing him from her grip.

"I do not 'chat,'" she said in a clear voice. "I provide riddles. If you solve a riddle, you live. If you do not, you die."

"Straightforward," Oedipus replied as he dusted himself off and got to his feet. "I like it."

The Sphinx only tensed her claws and bared her teeth. She couldn't wait to wipe the smug expression right off the man's face.

"Which creature has only one voice, but has four feet in the morning, two feet in the afternoon, and three feet at night?" the Sphinx asked.

Now Oedipus was a pretty clever guy, but he had never heard a riddle like this before. A creature with a changing amount of feet? That didn't even sound possible! He began to panic. What if he couldn't solve the riddle, after all? What if he died right here by this cranky monster with a snake tail?

Oedipus forced himself to take a deep breath. He thought carefully about the riddle and about what the question really meant. Maybe it didn't have to do with feet at all. After a while, he had the answer.

"A person!" he said. "People crawl on all fours as babies, walk on two legs as adults, and need a walking cane when they're old."

The Sphinx was shocked. She let out a gigantic roar that could be heard from every corner of Thebes. No one had ever solved the riddle before! But instead of letting him go as she had promised, the Sphinx asked Oedipus a second riddle.

"One more!" she screamed in his face.

"Well, ma'am, I believe the deal was that I would solve *one* riddle and then get to live."

The Sphinx simply snarled.

"Well, okay, we can try it your way," Oedipus said.

The Sphinx snarled again. "There are two sisters; one gives birth to the other, who in turn gives birth to the first. Who are they?"

Once again, Oedipus was stumped. But this time, he didn't panic. He walked around in circles, scratching his chin and wracking his brain.

Eventually, Oedipus offered an answer.

"I believe the answer to your riddle is: night and day. These two 'sisters' as you call them, turn into one another repeatedly. Night gives way to day, which then gives way to night once more."

Oedipus wasn't 100 percent sure, but he figured the Sphinx's cry of frustration was an indication that he had gotten the answer correct.

The Sphinx was so angry that she had been bested *twice* that she flew into a rage and destroyed herself, never to be seen again.

"Well, I guess that's done with," Oedipus said with a smile. "Let's go see about my new promotion."

When Oedipus returned to the heart of the city, he was greeted by thunderous applause. The people were amazed that he had defeated the monster that had haunted them for so long. King Creon held up his end of the bargain and offered Oedipus his throne.

"Anyone clever enough to solve those riddles deserves to be king," he said to Oedipus.

And with that, Oedipus took over as the ruler of Thebes, earning himself a legacy as a kind, intelligent, and just ruler. But he never solved another riddle again. He just didn't have the stomach for them anymore.

SOME LEGENDS SAY THAT THE SPHINX THREW HERSELF OFF A CLIFF; OTHERS SAY SHE DEVOURED HERSELF. BUT EITHER WAY, THE RIDDLE OF THE SPHINX HAD BEEN SOLVED.

This myth is a popular story in Greek mythology because it shows that you don't need huge muscles or heroic battle skills to fight a monster. Sometimes, the best weapon of all is your brain. Consider this a reminder to do your homework! After all, you never know when you'll meet a riddling monster with a hissing snake tail!

WHAT DO COMPUTERS EAT FOR A SNACK? MICROCHIPS! AND WE EAT THEM ONE BYTE AT A TIME! (YOU MAY NOW LOL.)

# GUIDE TO THE GREEKS!

This book is filled with lots of names—whether they're gods, goddesses, monsters, magical creatures, or a bunch of giants, it's a lot to remember! So in case you forget who somebody is (or have a tough time pronouncing those pesky giants' names), here's a handy-dandy, Oracle of Wi-Fi–approved guide to places, characters, and terms in these tales from Greek mythology.

**Achilles** (ah-KILL-eez): A famous Greek warrior who fought in the Trojan War, known for his overly sensitive heels.

**Acoetes** (ah-KOI-teez): A young pirate who had good god-detection skills.

**Acropolis** (ah-KRAA-puh-lus): A sacred and well-protected part of ancient Greek cities, usually built on a hill.

**Aeëtes** (eye-EE-teez): The king of Colchis who did not want to give up his precious Golden Fleece.

**Aegina** (ee-JEE-nuh): A beautiful nymph from Sisyphus's kingdom and the daughter of Asopus, the river god.

**Aegis** (EE-juhs): A shield made from the hide of Zeus's goat mother, Amalthea.

**Aeson** (AYE-ee-son): The king of Iolcus whose throne was stolen by his jealous brother, Pelias. Also named his son Jason (rhyming is fun!) just to keep everyone on their toes.

**Aglaea** (ah-GLAI-uh): The goddess who married Hephaestus and was actually very happy about it, unlike his prior wife, Aphrodite.

**Agora** (AH-gore-ah): A town square that served many purposes, including as a market and public forum.

**Ajax** (AY-jacks): The Greek hero who fought alongside Achilles in the Trojan War.

**Alcyone** (al-KOE-nee): A Greek princess happily married to Ceyx who was devastated after his death.

**Alectryon** (ah-LECK-tree-on): One of Ares' soldiers who was in desperate need of caffeine.

**Amalthea** (ah-MALL-thay-ah): Zeus's goat foster mother.

**Ambrosia** (am-BRO-see-ah): The food of the gods (shockingly, not pizza).

**Andromeda** (ann-DRO-meh-duh): The daughter of King Cepheus and Queen Cassiopeia. She agreed to sacrifice herself to a sea monster to save her kingdom, but ended up not getting eaten and instead married the handsome warrior Perseus.

**Aphrodite** (aff-row-DYE-tee): The goddess of love and beauty.

**Apollo** (uh-PAW-low): One of the most powerful Greek gods. He was known as the god of prophecy, music, poetry, archery, and healing. Twin to Artemis.

**Ares** (AIR-eez): Greek god of war and courage. Known for his hot head and quick temper.

**The Argo**: The famous ship that carried Jason and his Argonauts on their quest for the Golden Fleece.

**Argonauts** (ar-GOH-nots): The name for a band of heroes that helped Jason find the famous Golden Fleece. Argonauts alumni include Heracles, Perseus, and Atalanta—just to name a few.

**Argus Panoptes** (ARR-gus pan-OP-tayz): A giant with a hundred eyes who worked for Hera.

**Ariadne** (air-ee-ADD-knee): The daughter of King Minos and Queen Pasiphaë. Helped Theseus escape the Minotaur, only to be left behind on the island of Naxos. Later married the god Dionysus.

**Artemis** (AR-teh-miss): The Greek goddess of wild animals, the hunt, and childbirth. Twin to Apollo.

**Asclepius** (ask-LEAP-ee-us): The son of Apollo and prodigy healer of ancient Greece.

**Asopus** (AYE-soh-puss): A river god who was very concerned about his missing daughter.

**Atalanta** (at-uh-LAN-tuh): A hero who was raised by bears in the forest and ultimately became one of the country's best hunters.

**Athena** (ah-THEE-nah): The Greek goddess of wisdom, strategic warfare, and the arts.

**Atlas** (AT-lass): The Titan who bore the heavy weight of holding up the heavens and sky. Very sculpted biceps.

**Aulos** (OW-LOSS): A wind instrument that was often referred to as a "double flute."

**Calypso** (kuh-LIP-so): The sorceress who was stuck on an island all by herself. Big fan of Odysseus, not a big fan of Zeus.

**Cecrops** (KEH-krops): The King of Cecropia, the city now known as Athens.

**Centaur** (SEN-tar): A mythical creature with the body of a horse and the head and torso of a man.

**Cerberus** (SIR-burr-us): Hades' large three-headed dog that guarded the Underworld. Despite his scary appearance, we have it on record that he was a very good boy.

**Ceto** (KEE-tow): An ancient sea goddess and the mother to lots of scary creatures, including Medusa.

**Ceyx** (SEE-icks): A devoted husband who was killed in a ship-wreck after saying his marriage was as good as Zeus and Hera's.

**Charon** (CARE-on): The boatman who was responsible for ferrying souls across the Underworld's River Styx. Bit of a creepy job, but somebody had to do it.

**Charybdis** (kar-IB-diss): A giant whirlpool sea monster.

**Chimera** (kaye-MEER-uh): A fire-breathing monster with the head and body of a lion and the tail of a venomous serpent. It also had a goat head growing out of its midsection.

**Chiron** (KY-ron): The centaur famous for his wisdom and advice, who raised some of the most famous demigods and trained them to become great warriors.

**Circe** (KEER-key or SEER-see): Famous sorceress who created a potion that could grant immortality.

**Clytie** (klee-TEE-ee): A sea nymph who got her heart broken by Helios, the sun god.

**Creon** (KREE-on): The king of Thebes who was willing to give up the throne to whomever could get rid of the pesky Sphinx.

**Cronus** (CROW-nuss): The king of the Titans. He tried to get rid of his children, the future Olympians, by eating them. Don't worry, they got revenge.

Cyclops (SY-klops): One-eyed giants who helped the Olympians defeat the Titans. One is a cyclops. Two or more are called cyclopes (sy-klo-PEES). Now you know.

Danaë (dan-AH-ay): Perseus's beloved mother who caught the eye of a not-so-nice king.

Deino (DAY-no): The eldest of the three Gray Sisters, known for her negativity and doom-and-gloom attitude. Not so great at parties.

Demeter (duh-MEE-ter): The goddess of the harvest and agriculture. One of the original Olympians and Persephone's mother.

Dionysus (die-oh-NICE-us): The Olympian god of wine, pleasure, festivities, and big cats. (Yes, big cats.)

Echidna (EE-kid-nah): Half woman, half snake, and mama to the Sphinx.

Elatus (EL-ah-tuss): A wild centaur that tried to kill Heracles (rookie

mistake) and indirectly caused the great centaur Chiron's death.

Enyo (en-ee-AW): The baby Gray Sister who was said to represent horror itself. So kind of a party pooper.

Erebus (AIR-uh-bus): The god of darkness and hubby to Nyx.

Eros (EER-os): The god of love.

Euryale (you-REE-ah-lay): One of the Gorgon sisters.

Eurydice (you-RID-iss-see): The beloved wife of Orpheus who died a snake-related death.

The Fates: Also known as the Moirai (MOY-rye), these three sisters were the goddesses of fate. Each had a unique job in determining the destiny of humans living in the mortal world. They spun, measured, and eventually cut the thread of each human life.

The Furies: Deities of revenge and vengeance that punished evil souls.

Gaea (GUY-uh): The first being in Greek mythology, the goddess of Earth, and everyone's favorite great-great-great-great-great-great-great-great-great-great-great-great-great-great grandmother.

**Golden Fleece:** The golden wool of an enchanted winged ram located in the land of Colchis. Jason was forced to find it before he could take the throne back from his devious uncle.

**Gorgons** (GORE-gonz): Three very scary sisters with snakes for hair. The MVP was the infamous Medusa, who had the ability to turn people into stone if they looked at her.

**Gray Sisters:** Three old ladies (Deino, Pemphredo, and Enyo) who shared one eyeball, one tooth, and a whole lot of attitude.

**Hades** (HAY-deez): One of the original Olympians. After drawing the short straw (literally), he became king of the Underworld and presided over the dead.

**Harpies** (HARP-eez): Creatures with the body of a bird but the face of a human woman. Known for grabbing people from Earth and bringing them to the gods.

**Helen of Troy:** A beautiful mortal woman said to be the cause of the Trojan War.

**Helios** (HE-lee-os): The Titan god of the sun who was responsible for pulling it across the sky every day in his chariot.

**Hephaestus** (hef-FEST-us): The blacksmith of the gods who was in charge of making cool weapons.

**Hera** (HAIR-uh): One of the original Olympians and Zeus's wife. Known for her temper and cruel punishments, but her wisdom and bravery got the Olympians out of lots of sticky situations.

**Heracles** (HAIR-uh-kleez): The G.O.A.T. of Greek mythology, demigod, and big-time hero who earned his title by overcoming 12 famous trials to become immortal.

**Hermes** (HER-meez): The Greek god of wealth, trade, luck, and travel (just to name a few). Known for being the messenger and herald of the gods.

**Hesperides** (HESS-pear-ee-deez): Three beautiful nymphs who lived at the edge of the world and were guardians of Hera's garden and golden apples. Daughters of Atlas.

**Hippodamia** (hip-oh-DAM-ee-uh): A princess who married King Pirithous and had a very wild wedding.

**Io** (EYE-oh): A very unlucky priestess who worked for Hera and caught the eye of Zeus. Strong dislike for both cows and gadflies.

**Ixion** (ICKS-ee-on): A not-so-nice mortal who ultimately became the father of all centaurs. Big fan of clouds, especially those shaped like the goddess Hera.

**Jason:** The rightful ruler of Iolcus committed to taking back the throne from his evil Uncle Pelias. Went on a famous quest to look for the Golden Fleece.

**Kithara** (kih-THAR-ah): An advanced, guitar-like instrument often reserved for talented musicians during public performances.

**Kymbala** (kim-BALL-ah): Small cymbals played by the ancient Greeks.

**Laestrygonians** (LIE-stree-goh-knee-anz): A ferocious tribe of human-eating giants.

**Lapiths** (LAH-piths): A kingdom of humans in Thessaly. The Lapiths were not fans of centaurs.

**Leto** (LEE-tow): The mother to Apollo and Artemis. Hunted by a giant python before giving birth.

**Lotus-Eaters:** A bunch of chill people who chose to stay on a deserted island and eat hypnotic flowers all day long.

**Lyre** (LIE-er): A string instrument originally created by Hermes as a gift for his big bro, Apollo. Two of these frequently precede "pants on fire."

**M**

**Medea** (me-DEE-ya): The sorceress daughter of the king of Colchis who helped Jason on his quest for the Golden Fleece.

**Medusa** (med-OO-suh): A Gorgon with snakes for hair and a stare that could turn a person into stone.

**Metis** (MAY-tiss): A Titan who was Zeus's first wife and the mother of Athena.

**Midas** (MY-duss): A king famous for being overly obsessed with gold. Rewarded with a pair of donkey ears for stating an unpopular musical opinion.

**Minotaur** (ME-no-tar): The king of Crete's firstborn child who turned out to be a monster with the head and tail of a bull. The Minotaur was forced to live out his days trapped in the Labyrinth.

**Nectar:** The drink of the gods.

**Nymphs** (NIMFS): Female beings who were strongly associated with nature. They were not as powerful or immortal as gods, but they did live long, mystical lives.

**Nyx** (NICKS): The goddess of the darkness.

**Oceanids** (OH-she-ANN-ids): Power-ful water nymphs who lived in the sea.

**Odysseus** (oh-DISS-ee-us): King of Ithaca and a hero famous for his 10-year journey, or odyssey, home after fighting in the Trojan War.

**Oedipus** (ED-ee-puss): The man who was able to outsmart the Sphinx and become king of Thebes.

**Olympians** (oh-LIM-pee-uns): The six OG gods and goddesses named after their home on Mount Olympus: Hades, Hera, Hestia, Demeter, Poseidon, and Zeus.

**Oracle of Delphi** (DELF-eye): The most popular oracle in Greek mythology, who could communicate advice from the god Apollo.

**Oracles** (OR-uh-kulls): All-knowing, wise women who could receive divine guidance from the gods.

**Orion** (or-EYE-on): A famous hunter who fell in love with Artemis.

**Orpheus** (OR-fee-us): The musical prodigy who inherited his skill from his father, Apollo. Married Eurydice and went on an epic quest to rescue her from the Underworld.

**Orthus** (OR-thoos): A giant dog with two heads.

**Pan:** A flute-playing satyr with a happy-go-lucky attitude.

**Paris:** Not the city in France. Paris was a prince from Troy who fell in love with Helen of Troy and stole her away from Sparta. This act sparked the Trojan War. He also shot Achilles in the heel.

**Parthenon** (PAHR-thuh-non): A marble temple in Athens built to honor the goddess Athena.

**Patroclus** (PAH-troh-kluhs): Achilles' best friend and rumored soulmate.

**Peleus** (PEE-lee-us): The estranged husband to Thetis and father to Achilles.

**Pelias** (PEE-lee-ahs): Jason's evil uncle who killed his own brother to secure the throne. Sent Jason on a wild fleece chase to try to avoid giving up his power.

**Pelops** (PEE-lops): Tantalus's son who was brought back to life by Zeus. Strongly disliked stew.

**Pemphredo** (pem-FRAY-doh): The middle Gray Sister, representing panic and anxiety.

**Penelope** (pen-ELL-oh-pee): The wife of Odysseus.

**Persephone** (purr-SEH-phone-ee): Demeter's daughter and Hades' wife who embraced the role of queen of the Underworld.

**Perseus** (PURR-see-us): A famous warrior who killed the Gorgon Medusa and married the princess Andromeda.

**Philyra** (fuh-LIE-rah): The sea nymph and the mother of Chiron.

**Phineus** (FIN-ee-us): The very hungry ruler of Thrace whose appetite was always ruined by smelly harpy farts.

**Pholus** (FOE-luss): A wise centaur.

**Phorcys** (FOR-keyz): Dad of the Gorgons and the Gray Sisters.

**Pirithous** (pear-ee-THOO-us): The king and ruler of the Lapiths.

**Polydectes** (polly-DECK-tease): The king of Serifos who had a thing for Perseus's mother.

**Polyphemus** (pol-uh-FEE-muss): Poseidon's son and a cyclops with one—soon to be blinded—eye and a hatred for Nobody.

**Poseidon** (poh-SIGH-don): An OG Olympian and the god of the seas. Creator of horses, dolphins, and many other animals.

**Prometheus** (pro-ME-thee-us): One of the Titan brothers who was in charge of creating humankind. He broke the rules when he decided to give humans the gift of fire, and Zeus made him pay a painful price.

**Pythia** (PITH-ee-uh): Another term for the Oracle of Delphi.

**Pytho** (PIE-thoh): Gaea's snake offspring who was later killed by Apollo.

**Satyr** (SAY-ter): A woodland spirit that was part man, part goat.

**Scylla** (SKILL-uh): A sea monster created by Circe with six deadly heads and a serpentine tail. Guarded a narrow strait alongside Charybdis, the whirlpool.

**Semele** (SEM-ee-lee): Dionysus's mortal mother who died from one of Hera's tricks.

**Sirens** (SIGH-rens): Half-bird, half-human creatures that enchanted sailors to jump off their ships. The sirens then ate them for lunch.

**Sisyphus** (SISS-ee-fuss): A trickster who cheated death multiple times. Whenever anyone talks about pushing a boulder up a hill for all of eternity, they're talking about this guy.

**Sphinx** (SFINKS): A giant monster with the body of a lion, the head of a woman, wings of an eagle, a snake for a tail, and a penchant for riddles.

**Stheno** (STHEE-noh): Medusa's Gorgon sister.

**Styx** (STICKS): One of the most famous rivers in the Underworld that served as a border between the living and the dead.

**Syrinx** (SRINKS): A beautiful wood nymph who caught the eye of Pan, the satyr.

**T**

**Tantalus** (TAN-tah-lus): A really evil guy who made a disgusting stew. Punished for eternity by Zeus.

**Tartarus** (TAR-tar-us): A scary prison located in the deepest part of the Underworld.

**Thanatos** (THAN-nah-toss): The god of death.

**Theseus** (THEE-see-us): The son of Aegeus and the heir to the throne of Athens who stood up against the atrocities in Crete and succeeded in slaying the Minotaur.

**Thetis** (THEE-tis): A powerful sea nymph who was Achilles' mother. Firm believer in the value of strong heels.

**Thoosa** (THOOS-ah): The mother of the cyclopes.

**Tiresias** (tay-REE-see-us): A famous blind prophet who provided Odysseus with important guidance on his journey home.

**Titanomachy** (tie-ten-AH-ma-key): A 10-year battle between the Olympians and the Titans to see who would end up in charge of the Universe. Sometimes referred to as the War of the Titans.

**Titans** (TIE-tens): Some of the earliest beings in existence, and the ones who were in charge before the Olympians came along.

**Trojan War** (TROH-jahn): The famous war between Greece and Troy that went on for a really, really long time.

**Typhon** (TIE-fon): An incredibly tall giant with multiple dragon heads, snakes for legs, and enormous wings. And he could breathe fire.

**The Underworld:** The realm where souls and spirits go after death. Ruled by Hades and his wife, Persephone.

**Uranus** (OO-raw-noss): The god who was married to Gaea, the mother of the Universe. Didn't have much of a paternal instinct and locked up several of his children. This led to his son Cronus overthrowing him and taking away his power.

**Xenia** (ZEN-ee-ah): The Greek term for hospitality.

**Zeus** (ZOOS): An OG Olympian and the boss man of Greek mythology. The god of the sky and the ruler of the heavens.

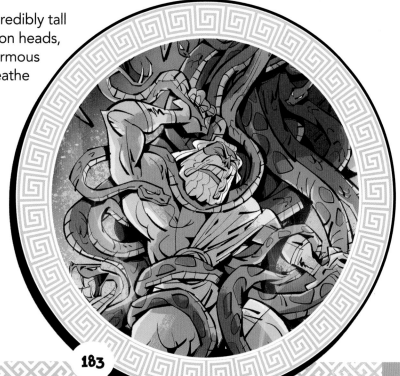

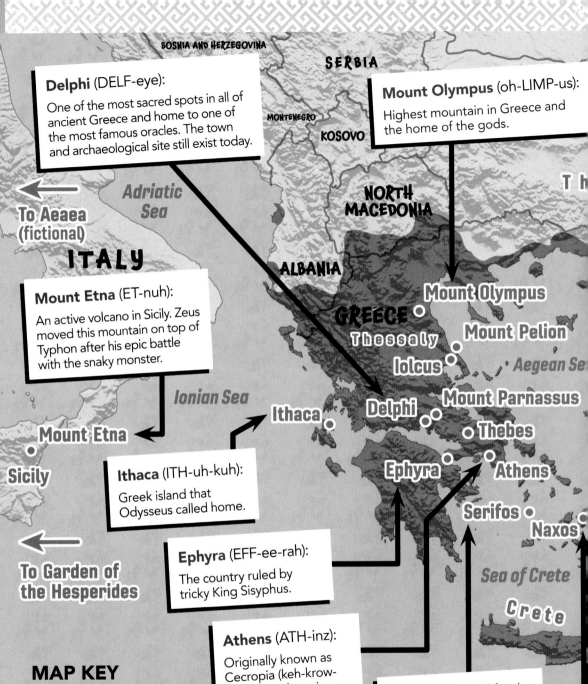

**Delphi** (DELF-eye):
One of the most sacred spots in all of ancient Greece and home to one of the most famous oracles. The town and archaeological site still exist today.

**Mount Olympus** (oh-LIMP-us):
Highest mountain in Greece and the home of the gods.

**Mount Etna** (ET-nuh):
An active volcano in Sicily. Zeus moved this mountain on top of Typhon after his epic battle with the snaky monster.

**Ithaca** (ITH-uh-kuh):
Greek island that Odysseus called home.

**Ephyra** (EFF-ee-rah):
The country ruled by tricky King Sisyphus.

**Athens** (ATH-inz):
Originally known as Cecropia (keh-krow-PEE-uh), Athens is a coastal city in the Mediterranean and the modern-day capital of Greece. (Named after Athena, not Poseidon. Aren't you glad it's not Poseidaho?)

**Serifos** (SAY-riff-fuss):
The island where Perseus and his mother, Danaë, lived before Perseus left on his quest to kill Medusa.

To Aeaea (fictional)

ITALY

To Garden of the Hesperides

BOSNIA AND HERZEGOVINA
SERBIA
MONTENEGRO
KOSOVO
NORTH MACEDONIA
ALBANIA
GREECE
Thessaly
Iolcus
Delphi
Ephyra
Athens
Thebes
Mount Parnassus
Mount Pelion
Mount Olympus
Serifos
Naxos
Sicily
Mount Etna
Ithaca
Adriatic Sea
Ionian Sea
Aegean Sea
Sea of Crete
Crete
T h

**MAP KEY**
- ○ Ancient point of interest
- ■ Area considered ancient Greece around 750 B.C.
- — Present-day boundary

| 0 | | 100 miles |
| 0 | | 100 kilometers |

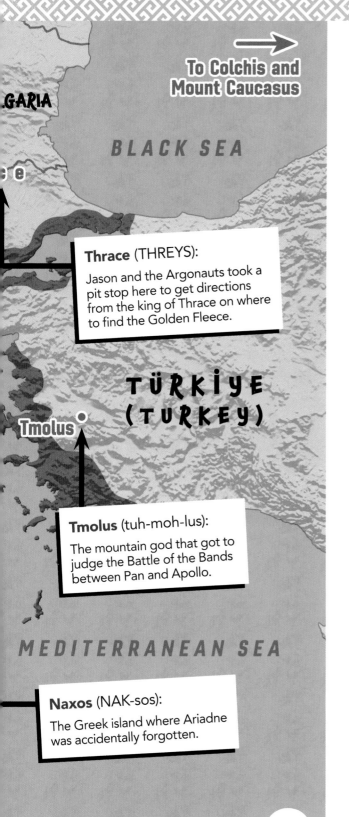

**To Colchis and Mount Caucasus**

.GARIA

*BLACK SEA*

**Thrace** (THREYS):
Jason and the Argonauts took a pit stop here to get directions from the king of Thrace on where to find the Golden Fleece.

**TÜRKİYE (TURKEY)**

Tmolus

**Tmolus** (tuh-moh-lus):
The mountain god that got to judge the Battle of the Bands between Pan and Apollo.

*MEDITERRANEAN SEA*

**Naxos** (NAK-sos):
The Greek island where Ariadne was accidentally forgotten.

**Colchis** (KOL-kiss): A faraway land that was home to the most famous blanket of all time: the Golden Fleece.

**Garden of the Hesperides** (HESS-pear-ee-deez): A garden that belonged to the goddess Hera and was tended to by three beautiful nymphs called the Hesperides.

**Iolcus** (ee-YOL-kuss): The hero Jason's country and home turf.

**Mount Caucasus** (KAW-kuh-sus): A famous mountain that Prometheus was chained to after disobeying Zeus and giving fire to mankind. Also home to a rather hungry eagle that helped himself to Prometheus's liver for breakfast.

**Mount Parnassus** (pahr-NAS-us): Home to the Temple of Apollo in Delphi.

**Mount Pelion** (PEE-lee-on): A mountain in Thessaly that was home to the wisest centaur in Greece, Chiron.

**Thessaly** (THESS-all-ee): Located in northern Greece, this wooded, mountainous region was home to centaurs and a kingdom of humans called the Lapiths.

# INDEX

# ABOUT THE PODCAST

*Greeking Out* is an original podcast from National Geographic Kids that retells the most epic tales from Greek mythology. Perfect for the whole family, this audio storytelling experience is voiced by master storyteller and 30-year radio veteran Kenny Curtis, while the hilarious and snarky Oracle of Wi-Fi breaks in with facts and tidbits on ancient Greek history and culture and beyond. The podcast also takes field trips to farther-flung locations to explore mythology and folklore from other incredible cultures—from ancient Mesopotamia to the Inca Empire to India and to sub-Saharan Africa. Each 20-minute episode thrills listeners with bloodthirsty monsters, powerful gods and goddesses, unlikely heroes, awkward family dynamics, amazing animals, and, of course, the greatest stories ever told.

AVAILABLE WHEREVER YOU GET YOUR PODCASTS!

# PHOTO CREDITS

All artwork by Javier Espila unless otherwise noted below:

17, David/Adobe Stock; 18, Andrea Izzotti/Shutterstock; 19, Katja Forster/Shutterstock; 22, Tandem Stock/Adobe Stock; 22-23 (CTR), kamnuan/Shutterstock; 23 (UP LE), Andy Rouse/ Nature Picture Library; 23 (UP RT), robertharding/Adobe Stock; 23 (LO), Dudarev Mikhail/ Adobe Stock; 33, VERSUSstudio/Shutterstock; 38, mahir ates/Alamy Stock Photo; 45, Sebastian Kaulitzki/Shutterstock; 49, TTstudio/Adobe Stock; 50, Tomas Marek/Adobe Stock; 51 (UP), elgreko/Adobe Stock; 51 (CTR), sea and sun/Adobe Stock; 51 (LO), DAC/Adobe Stock; 56, Andrey_Kuzmin/Shutterstock; 62 (UP), Jùn hòushēng/Adobe Stock; 62 (LO), Katecat/Adobe Stock; 73, idal/iStockphoto; 76, The Picture Art Collection/Alamy Stock Photo; 77 (UP), Azoor Photo/Alamy Stock Photo; 77 (LO LE), ArtInfo/Bridgeman Images; 77 (LO RT), Terese Loeb Kreuzer/Alamy Stock Photo; 83, Inge Johnsson/Alamy Stock Photo; 90, MAREK MIS/Science Source; 92, DEAN TREML/Stringer/Getty Images; 98, GrashAlex/Shutterstock; 100 (LE), PRISMA ARCHIVO/Alamy Stock Photo; 100 (RT), Hercules Milas/Alamy Stock Photo; 101 (UP), WH_Pics/Shutterstock; 101 (CTR), afrumgartz/Adobe Stock; 101 (LO LE), Fotos 593/Adobe Stock; 101 (LO RT), MET/BOT/Alamy Stock Photo; 113, Mike/Adobe Stock; 118, Razvan Marian Vlasceanu/Alamy Stock Photo; 124, Album/Alamy Stock Photo; 125 (UP), Science Source; 125 (CTR), Lebrecht Music & Arts/Alamy Stock Photo; 125 (LO), Album/Alamy Stock Photo; 131, Historic Collection/Alamy Stock Photo; 146, Patryk Kosmider/ Adobe Stock; 150-151, NG Maps; 154, Matthijs Kuijpers/Alamy Stock Photo; 164, SciePro/Adobe Stock; 170, Dan Breckwoldt/Dreamstime

This book is dedicated to our friend Diane. Some folks knew her as Dr. Diane Harris Cline, some folks knew her as "Lady Cline"—but we all knew her kind laugh, the joy she took in her work, and her passion for stories like these. Among many other things, she was a mother, a wife, a professor, a Fulbright scholar, and a guiding light for all things *Greeking Out*. Diane currently resides in Elysium, where she spends her days snacking on ambrosia and lovingly watching the folly of foolish mortals like us. —K.C. & J.H.

Copyright © 2024 National Geographic Partners, LLC.

All rights reserved. Reproduction of the whole or any part of the contents without written permission from the publisher is prohibited.

NATIONAL GEOGRAPHIC and Yellow Border Design are trademarks of the National Geographic Society, used under license.

Since 1888, the National Geographic Society has funded more than 14,000 research, conservation, education, and storytelling projects around the world. National Geographic Partners distributes a portion of the funds it receives from your purchase to National Geographic Society to support programs including the conservation of animals and their habitats. To learn more, visit natgeo.com/info.

For more information, visit nationalgeographic.com, call 1-877-873-6846, or write to the following address:

National Geographic Partners, LLC
1145 17th Street NW
Washington, DC 20036-4688 U.S.A.

More for kids from National Geographic: natgeokids.com

*National Geographic Kids* magazine inspires children to explore their world with fun yet educational articles on animals, science, nature, and more. Using fresh storytelling and amazing photography, *Nat Geo Kids* shows kids ages 6 to 14 the fascinating truth about the world—and why they should care. natgeo.com/subscribe

For rights or permissions inquiries, please contact National Geographic Books Subsidiary Rights: bookrights@natgeo.com

Art directed and designed by Sanjida Rashid
Editorial by WonderLab Group, LLC

Hardcover ISBN: 978-1-4263-7627-6
Reinforced library binding ISBN: 978-1-4263-7713-6

The publisher would like to thank: Kenny Curtis and Jillian Hughes, authors and researchers, and Javier Espila, illustrator. Book team: Katie Moore, senior editor; Lori Epstein, photo manager; Rick Castle, expert reviewer; Molly Reid, production editor; David Marvin, associate designer.

Printed in the United States of America
24/WOR/1

# GREEK MYTHOLOGY
## KNOW-IT-ALL?

**Since you've read *Greeking Out*, you're well on your way. But there's more to discover!** This Weird But True! book, full of fun facts, maps, and stories, is a handy guide to who's who and what's what in the amazing and a-MUSE-ing mythological world of the ancient Greeks.

## AVAILABLE WHEREVER BOOKS ARE SOLD
Discover more at natgeokids.com

© 2024 National Geographic Partners, LLC